THE
BUSINESS
CONTINUITY
OPERATING
SYSTEM

Praise for the Author

"To continuity professionals, I recommend two things: add Brian to speed dial and keep this book handy. I'm lucky to access the Castellan team's expertise, troubleshooting, and enthusiasm to amplify and augment our efforts. The approach is flexible, intuitive, and dare I say, fun. This isn't an out-of-the-box, one-size-fits-most solution that checks a box to meet a requirement. You get as much as you put into it. The system considers culture, capacity, and creativity. A must-read, dog-ear, bookmark, and highlight guide."

—Jenny Borgosz Jolly

"Hats off to Brian Zawada's BCOS book! I laughed out loud at the end of Chapter One as I too, have experienced going from hero to goat as a business continuity manager! Brian's book contains real-world issues that business continuity professionals must manage and solve. No matter where you are in your resiliency career, take advantage of the many pearls of wisdom and lessons learned planted in the rich ground of the BCOS."

—Jean D. Rowe

"We operate in an extremely stressful environment and at times it is hard to balance it all. Luckily, I have had the opportunity to work with outstanding consultants and tool sets. Specifically, Brian Zawada and the BC software tool his organization provides. Brian engineered the strategic direction from a BC/DR practitioner's perspective, creating BC policy and standard operating procedures. These fundamentals put us on the path of success even though, as Senior Director of BC Services for a Fortune 5, I and my team were struggling. Brian was able to incorporate the BCOS into the environment and significantly improve the program. Bottom line, Brian and BCOS took us several levels upward in maturity from a program perspective while improving morale!"

—Raymond Seid

"Brian and I first met in 2016 at the International Standards Symposium in Morioka, Japan. Since then, we have collaborated on new and revised standards, debated ideas, reflected on our consulting experiences, and considered the future of BC and Resilience. I have seen how Brian's management and thought leadership has transformed his own business and protected the businesses of his clients. As a result, I have tremendous respect for Brian and his opinion. He has become more than an industry educator; Brian Zawada has become an international BC influencer."

—**Saul Midler,** FBCI (Hon)

"Brian has been both a professional colleague and a trusted advisor for many years. We met prior to the establishment of his consulting firm. This long-term relationship has given me insight into both who Brian is and how he conducts business. His approach to continuity is pragmatic. Brian's ability to simplify business continuity concepts down to the most essential components allows for him to communicate with all levels within an organization effectively. Brian's expertise in the risk and resilience fields is an asset to his clients and the industry."

—**Tonya T York,** MBCP, MBCI
DRII Lifetime Achievement Award Winner

THE
BUSINESS
CONTINUITY
OPERATING
SYSTEM

WHAT **THE BEST** DO DIFFERENTLY
TO ACHIEVE SUCCESS

BRIAN ZAWADA

THE
BUSINESS
CONTINUITY
OPERATING
SYSTEM

WHAT **THE BEST** DO DIFFERENTLY
TO ACHIEVE SUCCESS

To contact the author, Brian Zawada, visit castellanbc.com

To contact the publisher, Gravitas Press, visit GravitasPress.com

Printed in the United States of America
ISBN 9781735943527

Book Strategist & Coach: Bonnie Budzowski, Gravitas Press
Copyeditor: Brenda Quinn
Interior Design: Melissa Farr, Back Porch Creative

Contents

Preface

Business continuity is a relatively intuitive, simple topic that often gets over-complicated in its implementation. Let me try to explain without using an industry definition: *Business continuity is all about trying to keep the organization's mission from being disrupted and, if something bad happens, implementing an established plan to return to normal as quickly as possible.* It's that simple!

But again, those responsible for business continuity in their organizations over-complicate the approach to choosing and implementing solutions that prevent and/or respond to disruption. They also struggle to sustain the planning effort over time.

In today's business climate, we must compete for the attention of all stakeholders. We must be able to create energy among the different program participants that do their part in helping the organization get to the right business continuity outcomes.

Those outcomes are the strategies that the organization can employ to respond and recover successfully when faced with a disruption, clarify and focus on what to protect, and create confidence among those that benefit from business continuity.

As a consultant who has worked with hundreds of organizations over the years, I've seen all kinds of problems get in the way of organizations achieving the right level of resilience.

Based on my experiences and observations, I decided to write a book that demystifies the topic of business continuity management and provides guidance on how to avoid the most common mistakes. I wanted this book to help sustain the planning effort, with a focus on really connecting business continuity to the strategy of the organization. Plenty of books and white papers already address methodology, so I cover that at a fairly high level. Instead, I chose to focus on the areas that cause confusion, create unnecessary complexity, and result in poor performance. I believe that lack of focus and engagement are the two primary root causes of poor performance.

The solution to these two problems, and others, is something we call the Business Continuity Operating System, or BCOS. The BCOS model is a set of processes and tools that the Castellan team developed over many years, and I'm eager to share it with you, the reader.

I personally learn best through stories, so I decided that a fictitious story or case study would be an ideal way to introduce the BCOS. This story depicts the use of the BCOS in action, rather than introduce it using theory. If you are not a fan of stories, don't worry; I follow the fictional case study with an explicit description of BCOS.

Chapter 1 begins by telling the story of Michael Taylor's journey in building a business continuity program at Felder Corporation. It reveals how he designed, implemented, and evolved business continuity for Felder and discovered the BCOS.

If you are new to business continuity, I suspect Michael's story will resonate right away. If you are reading this book with considerable business continuity experience, or if you're operating a mature business continuity program, I invite you to read the story and look for concepts that you can apply to improve focus and engagement. If you are experienced but something seems to be missing, I think you'll also find that the BCOS will improve your job satisfaction.

Regardless of your experience level, I hope that after reading this book, you too will achieve successful outcomes and the right level of resilience for your organization.

The book's table of contents, together with 'call-out boxes' (which summarize key takeaways and offer additional tools or content outside of the book), will direct you to core BCOS topics that may help overcome a common area of struggle in your organization. The fable starts in Chapter 1, but if you want a little more background on Felder Corporation, the fictitious company that's covered in the book, you can read Appendix I. If you want a little more background on Felder's leadership team and the characters in the fable, review Appendix II.

At any point, I invite you to move beyond the story and review the details of the BCOS, beginning in Chapter 30. Starting there, I explicitly introduce the core elements of the BCOS.

One last point. Beginning in Chapter 11, you will see graphics pointing to the BCOS implementation phase, as well as a notional timeline for the Year-One implementation. These graphics are there just to help clarify where Michael is in his journey. Please note the timeline is truly notional, in that a Year-One implementation is dependent on organizational size, complexity, engagement, and resource availability.

I hope the story and the content are both enjoyable and helpful as you work to protect your organization and enable it to continue regardless of circumstance.

– Brian Zawada

Acknowledgments

My appreciation to the Castellan team that delivers incredible value to our clients every day, and who contributed tirelessly to the design of the Business Continuity Operating System (BCOS) and its underlying processes and tools (as well as to this book!).

To our clients, partners, and friends, who provided the inspiration—and the feedback—that led to the BCOS innovation and this book.

And to the many business coaches, mentors, and authors that introduced key business practices that equally applied to Castellan, as well as to the design, implementation, and continual improvement of business continuity program management.

In particular, I acknowledge the EOS Worldwide organization and Gino Wickman, the creators of the Entrepreneurial Operating System (EOS). In our journey to implement EOS at Castellan, we quickly discovered the many benefits that EOS principles can offer to help organizations achieve the right level of resilience.

Where I Dropped the Ball

After about three minutes of reading the business continuity plan template I handed him, my boss, Andrew Preston, the CFO of Felder Corporation, took off his glasses, paused, and looked me squarely in the eye. "I need to be honest with you, Michael, I think you've missed the mark on this. I don't believe this will come close to meeting our clients' expectations or those of our senior leadership team."

He continued, "I'm actually disappointed in the recommendation you've made. You know how hard we've been working to get Paulsen as a new customer, and this plan you've put together simply isn't going to work for them, or us."

It felt like the air left the room. Nine weeks into my new role with Felder, I felt I hadn't really connected with my new employer. Even worse, I had dropped the ball with my boss. As I struggled with a response, he continued, "You're right that we need a plan. But having a plan document alone isn't going to make us any more prepared or resilient. We need to address real issues with our ability to persevere following the onset of a major disaster. For example, could we keep producing product without SAP? Is SAP even critical? What about replacing equipment at a damaged site? How about our key suppliers—what happens if they fail?"

Andrew continued, "I don't think your plan template tells us where we need to be or where we need to go with business continuity. The plan, or plans, need a specific set of objectives and a strategy on how we would recover when faced with a wide range of threats. Perhaps more importantly, I just reviewed a draft copy of the contract that we're planning to execute with Paulsen. They not only mandated that we have a business continuity plan, but they also mandated a number of other requirements, including a business impact analysis (BIA), exercises, and employee training. They even asked that we model our program based on an ISO standard."

Andrew handed me a piece of paper, which included the business continuity clause in the draft contract between Felder and Paulsen.

I read it, looked up, and apologized for missing the mark. I promised a more thoughtful approach and outcome. And then I left his office.

As I walked back to my office, I got angry all over again. I didn't want this business continuity assignment. After all, I came to Felder with the promise to work on something far more strategic—enterprise risk management.

By the time I got back to my office, I had just about convinced myself I should call my old employer and ask for my consulting job back. In my frustration, I made a call to my wife, and she talked me off the ledge, as she often does, and I calmed down a bit. But I still didn't want to lead the business continuity project.

Chapter 2

How I Got into This Mess

The nine weeks I'd been at Felder seemed to fly by. I'd been hired to mature Felder's risk management program, with my initial focus on fixing the insurance program for a rapidly growing contract manufacturing organization focused on biotech products and processes. At the same time, I saw my role at Felder as an incredible opportunity to mature and expand risk management into something far more strategic for this company. The CFO and COO both agreed with me.

For the seven years prior to joining Felder, I'd been in a consulting role, helping organizations design and implement enterprise risk management programs that focus on a wide range of risks and opportunities. But consulting wasn't enough for me. I missed being part of an organization, seeing problems past the initial solution, and getting deep into continuous improvement.

For a few years now, I've had a mentor who was also a client, Shannon Carter. She's Felder's COO and the one that introduced me to the opportunity at Felder. In addition to my personal desire to get embedded in a company rather than serving more than half a dozen organizations at a time, I found the idea of building something from scratch intriguing, especially for a rapidly growing company like Felder. Plus, my wife and I saw the job at Felder as a way of significantly decreasing my travel time.

Felder Corporation is a contract manufacturer of pharmaceutical products. Universities, research labs, and even large pharmaceutical companies engage Felder to produce pharmaceutical products on their behalf. Some of the larger, global pharmaceutical companies are Felder's customers; two of them alone account for 45 percent of Felder's $6B in annual revenue. Founded in 1990 and having gone public in 2003, Felder has performed in a profitable manner for five straight years, with operating margins averaging 18 percent. Over the past eighteen months, with the acquisition of one of its larger competitors, Belview Pharmaceuticals, Felder is operating close to capacity and is facing several key decisions regarding expansion.

Felder does not own any of the patents or formularies for the products it produces for clinical trials and commercial purposes. Rather, its customers are the ones investing and testing modern therapeutics. In 2015, Felder began offering additional services to its customers. Chief among them are process development (helping to create methods to develop, test, and commercialize therapies), adverse events reporting (helping to capture and manage when a patient has a negative reaction to a therapy), and clinical trials management processes (the controlled testing of therapies among a select number of patients). To date, two customers have taken advantage of these services, which are run out of the Cleveland, Ohio, headquarters.

The more I learned about Felder, the more exciting this opportunity seemed to me. After extensive interviews, I joined the company. I showed up with a specific game plan to transform Felder's approach to risk management.

Now, as I reflected on my first nine weeks at Felder, I realized I wasn't making too much progress on getting people excited about enterprise risk management (ERM). I'd held meetings to introduce the topic, explain roles and responsibilities, and even show how managing risk would evolve over the next five years, but there didn't seem to be much excitement (other than mine). I'd noticed attendance waning significantly week after week and had started to get frustrated. But I had no idea why. I'd never had this problem as a consultant.

Because I was at a loss, I set up a meeting with Shannon titled 'Mentoring Advice.' She accepted, and we met in the Felder cafeteria. I recapped the issue and asked for her advice, wondering whether the organization was really committed to enterprise risk management.

I could tell Shannon wanted to tell me something important. She paused before starting.

"Michael, you and I have worked together for a number of years. You know me to be straightforward, so here I go. I've attended two of your 'Introducing ERM' meetings, and to me, they were kind of boring, more theoretical than practical about how ERM might benefit Felder and its leaders. As I reflected on the second meeting, I found myself wondering whether you even have a solid grasp of what Felder does."

Ouch.

I was confused. Of course I didn't know the ins and outs of what Felder does. I had just joined the company, and I was busy trying to make an impact as a risk management specialist. There would be plenty of time to learn the business later. Why would Shannon criticize me for jumping into my job with both feet?

She continued, "Even before you scheduled this meeting, our CFO approached me and expressed a concern about how to get ERM off the ground. I won't share his ideas with you right now, but I think he's got an idea or two on how he wants you to learn more about the business, which he—and I—think is essential to get ERM to a good place."

When I started to ask Shannon for more information on these ideas, she shot me down. She told me to set up a meeting with the CFO as soon as possible because it would be better to hear it straight from him.

Concerned that the CFO, Andrew Preston, who is also my boss, was dissatisfied in some way with my performance, I scheduled the meeting with him. That was the day that my role at Felder changed quite a bit. I think it was a Wednesday.

Andrew invited Shannon, Jacob Cunningham, our general counsel, and Steve Henry, our head of business development, to the meeting.

Andrew started the meeting, looking my way. "Steve, Shannon, and I met last week, and we have a pretty significant growth opportunity that we want to take advantage of. Paulsen, one of the largest and fastest-growing pharmaceutical companies in the world, is interested in leveraging our contract manufacturing capabilities for two of its products that are close to receiving FDA approval following successful clinical trials. Paulsen is not a current client, and Steve's been targeting them heavily for twenty-four months now. Steve came to me yesterday because one of their requirements is a strong business continuity capability."

Steve continued, "Right. All their other requirements are straightforward, and quite honestly, I think we meet some, if not most, already. Based on my conversation with Jacob, business continuity is the one that concerns me. Paulsen doesn't want to pay for multisite manufacturing capability right now, but they want to know that we have plans to recover an affected manufacturing location's capacity in the event of a major catastrophic event. Given the expectation that we would place their manufacturing in Carolina, Puerto Rico, they are concerned about the threat of hurricanes."

Shannon added, "They are demanding some specific language in their contract for business continuity, and none of us are comfortable with their request unless we have a strategy to meet their business continuity expectations. To add to what Steve has already said, they want business continuity capability, not only for the manufacturing processes, but also for anything else that supports their contract manufacturing. They want us to follow a specific standard, and they want the right to audit us periodically, with penalty clauses for noncompliance. This is far more than what our existing customers have asked for."

"That's where we need you, Michael," added Andrew. "As part of our broader risk management program, we'd like to place the responsibility for designing and implementing the business continuity program with you. We've talked about this with Corey (Felder's CEO), and we all agree it's time to look at this effort strategically and for the company as a whole, rather than just for a new customer.

I want you to give this some thought and come back to us in a month or so with a high-level approach to tackling the business continuity program design and implementation. We indicated to Paulsen that we could have a business continuity program established in eighteen months, and they seem to be okay with that."

I was immediately uncomfortable, maybe annoyed more than anything. Shannon told me that she and Andrew had a plan to help me understand the Felder business, not add more responsibility.

"I don't mean to push back," I said, "but I'm new to the organization. Plus, you've given me a number of objectives around improving insurance and enterprise risk management, and perhaps most important, I have very little experience with business continuity. Are you sure I'm the right person?"

Andrew interrupted and held up his hand. "I understand your concern, Michael. But for right now, we think you're the best fit. Risk is the closest thing to business continuity, and with my support and knowledge of the company, I think I can direct you to the appropriate areas of the business and other leaders and subject matter experts. We talked about putting this under Anne (Felder's CIO), but we don't want it to be perceived as just an IT risk effort. We talked about putting it in Shannon's organization, but we don't want it to be singularly focused on manufacturing either. And we talked about Sara's organization (head of Felder's internal audit department), but she pointed out that she audits controls, she doesn't own them—and I agree. So, we'll work through your time constraints, but netting this customer, and getting this specific risk under control, is critical."

He paused for a moment and then continued, "I think you met with Shannon recently and she shared some feedback with you about the perceptions of our new ERM program. She and I are both in agreement that tackling business continuity might help you learn more about the business, which will help with ERM."

I was skeptical, or at the very least, I didn't understand that last point. I didn't see how fully understanding the business was critical to getting risks under control. While that knowledge would come with time, I had to deal with the risks now.

That day, my original five-phase game plan to strategically manage risk grew to six, and according to the executive team, business continuity moved decisively to the top of the list. To me, however, it was a distant sixth, and that's how I planned to prioritize it. I didn't realize that decision would be to my own detriment.

Chapter 3

Now What?

I went back to my office and sat down, feeling a mixture of anger and annoyance. I'd spent years bouncing between multiple clients, and I had been looking forward to a more focused job. Is this shifting focus characteristic of Felder? When Shannon approached me about considering this position and I shared my professional goals, she assured me I would be happy at Felder. Well, two months in, I'm not. What's next? Are they going to ask me to get involved in compliance, facilities management, or the new program management office?

I knew *of* business continuity (or at least I thought I did). The subject comes up all the time with insurance carriers as they look to underwrite property and business interruption insurance. Ten years ago, I was part of a team that did some work focused on IT disaster recovery, which is the term used to prepare for a disruption to IT services such as servers, applications, network communications, telecommunications, and electronic records. Over the years, I also attended presentations at conferences on the topic. But I never had responsibility for it, and I certainly hadn't started a program from scratch! And I didn't want to.

Beyond my limited experience and lack of desire, I didn't have the time for this assignment. Despite Andrew's assurances that he would help me prioritize my work, I am a team of one, and I have insurance renewals starting in six weeks. Plus, I owe internal audit my proposed design of the ERM program at the beginning of the next quarter. ERM is something I know and want to do. One thing's for sure—it will take me weeks to come up with something definitive to share with Sara Terrence, director of our internal audit department.

Regardless, I resigned myself to making sure I met Andrew's expectations when it came to business continuity. Perhaps deep in the back of my mind, I was looking for a quick solution to get this business continuity thing behind me.

Just as with everything new I tackle, I started with a Google search. I did a search for 'business continuity planning' and got something like six million results. There were magazines, professional associations, consulting organizations, and even software to help. I found references to standards and, for certain industries, regulations mandating business continuity. I started reading.

To me, the obvious result of business continuity is a plan. That seemed easy enough. If I have a plan to describe how Felder would respond to different threats, that would be good enough, right? From what I'd read, customers often ask for copies of a plan, so if I wrote a high-level plan that could be shared with Paulsen, especially one that focused on how we would respond to a hurricane, we should be good.

I did another search for 'business continuity plan template.' One of the industry magazines had a site for templates. I registered with them and created an account on their website, which gave me access. There were dozens of examples, some titled 'crisis management plan template,' others titled 'business continuity plan template,' 'business recovery plan template,' 'contingency plan template,' 'crisis communications plan template,' or 'emergency response plan template.' The templates seemed similar, so I stuck with the term that Andrew used, 'business continuity plan template.'

The template seemed straightforward. It referred to an initial response process, a situation assessment form, a business continuity team to lead the response, checklists for evacuation, personnel accountability, media communications, and how to determine an effective method to recover following the onset of a disruption. The content all seemed easy to update, and I began to wonder why I would need eighteen months to tackle this assignment. If I had a plan completed

For all locations, I assumed this documentation would satisfy Paulsen and meet any of their contractual requirements.

This became my approach. I would create a plan for each of the following Felder locations:

- Independence, Ohio (addressing the corporate headquarters)
- Carolina, Puerto Rico
- New Brunswick, New Jersey
- Concord, California
- Quincy, Massachusetts
- Portland, Oregon
- Cork, Ireland

Because the Carolina site is the main driver for this effort, and their #1 threat is hurricanes, I thought I'd better do another search for 'hurricane response procedures.' Sure enough, lots of examples came back, and I downloaded a few sets of procedures that I could add to the Carolina plan once I created it.

As I was reviewing some of the plan templates, other information emerged, including articles and templates for things such as risk assessment, threat assessment, BIA, and policies. I dismissed these as unnecessary for Felder for several reasons:

1. I know the threats we need to focus on (e.g., hurricanes).
2. I don't need to understand the impact to initiate business continuity. I was told to initiate planning by our senior leadership team and one of their customers.
3. Based on my understanding, Felder is not a policy-driven organization. Corey and Andrew are the drivers, so I moved past the policy considerations, too.

In sum, a lot of stuff out there looked like a bunch of bureaucracy designed for banks. Much of what I read appeared to introduce too much structure for a company like ours—we needed to move faster.

By the end of that day, I felt I had a good game plan and was a lot less worried about balancing my work priorities. I felt I'd be able to knock out business continuity before the end of the quarter! Maybe I hadn't made a mistake in taking the job at Felder after all. Something was still bothering me, though. Why did Andrew and Shannon think business continuity would help me learn more about the business—and why was that so important right now? I still wasn't connecting the dots.

I created a short memo summarizing my ideas (something like a project charter), started work on a business continuity plan for the Carolina site so I had something to show Andrew, and scheduled a meeting with him for the following Tuesday to review my approach and get his approval. Thirty-six hours later, I had all the materials together for Tuesday and returned my attention to the project I figured was most important, the insurance renewal.

Chapter 4

Hiccup
(That Tuesday)

As you know, Andrew was less than pleased with the material I presented. I'll never forget how he took off his glasses, looked me squarely in the eyes, and said, "I need to be honest with you, Michael, I think you've missed the mark on this. I don't believe this will come close to meeting our clients' expectations or those of our senior leadership team."

He expressed his disappointment as well as his expectations. "I don't think your plan template tells us where we need to be or where we need to go with this. The plan, or plans, needs a specific set of objectives and a strategy on how we would recover when faced with a wide range of threats. Perhaps more importantly, we need to develop something that satisfies Paulsen. They not only mandated we develop a plan, but they also mandated a number of other requirements, which include a BIA, exercises, and employee training, and they even asked that we model our program based on an ISO standard."

As I was preparing to leave the office with my tail between my legs, Andrew handed me a piece of paper, which included the business continuity clause in the draft contract between Felder and Paulsen.

He then casually threw me a lifeline: "By the way, have you met Ben Campbell? He's a manager in quality."

I responded that I hadn't met Ben yet, and Andrew continued, "I recall that Ben had a role in developing Creden's business continuity program prior to joining us three years ago. I'm sure he will have some good advice for you. Why don't you set up some time to meet with him, review the draft contract, and then let's reconnect next Friday with a revised approach. Does that work?"

I returned a weak nod and left his office. As I returned to my office and got over some of my anger and frustration, I realized that I had made an obvious mistake. Beyond looking for a shortcut to get this task done, I had made a bad assumption that business continuity is all about the plan; there was obviously much more to it. Not only that, I had failed to review the wording in the contract that my work was meant to address. Truth be told, I think subconsciously I didn't want to take this assignment seriously. And my new boss called me out on it.

After calming down even more, and remembering that I could be traveling 180 days a year, I partially resigned myself to getting this assignment right.

I sat down at my desk and reviewed the draft contract. Andrew was right; Paulsen was expecting far more than a plan. They not only stipulated their expectations regarding the outcomes of the planning process, but they also expected us to design a full business continuity program based on an ISO standard, ISO 22301. They even mandated certain maximum downtime expectations in case any of the business processes that directly or indirectly support our work for them were to fail. Paulsen even described their expectations regarding the continuity of our supply chain.

I settled—actually slumped—into my desk chair. I was feeling overwhelmed and a little down on myself. I needed to redeem myself with my boss and get this assignment under control. I barely knew where to begin. I sure hoped this guy Ben would be able to help.

Chapter 5

My Coach Ben
(the Next Day)

I got on Ben's calendar for the next day. With six business days to prepare for my next meeting with Andrew, I had more work than I originally anticipated.

I met Ben at 9 a.m. in a conference room on the third floor. I arrived a few minutes early, and he arrived right on time. Ben seemed somewhat reserved, but he had a warm smile. We shook hands, introduced ourselves, and sat down. We discussed our backgrounds and experiences at Felder. As Andrew had mentioned, Ben had come from Creden, one of our competitors, a little over three years prior.

During our introductions, I learned that Ben had been looking for a career change as he left Creden, and since his arrival in our quality organization, he'd moved rapidly into management and now had responsibility for quality engineering and quality control across all our manufacturing locations. He mentioned he had wanted something different because his work in business continuity was time-consuming. I think I closed my eyes to count to ten because Ben had just inadvertently reminded me that there was no way I could do this task well with all my other responsibilities.

As Ben continued introducing himself, I realized that Andrew had downplayed Ben's business continuity experience. Ben had not only designed his former employer's business continuity program from scratch, he had also managed it for ten years, taking the program from next to nothing to something resembling a world-class program.

I explained my situation to Ben, starting with my meeting with Andrew, Shannon, and Jacob last week, Paulsen's expectations, Corey's broader expectations, and my research to date on the topic of business continuity. I told him about my disastrous meeting with Andrew, and Andrew's recommendation that I reach out to Ben for advice. "Ben, to be honest, I really don't want this assignment. I came to Felder to focus on other things, not a new program that doesn't align with my experience."

Ben asked, "Did you tell that to Andrew and the others?"

"Kind of," I responded. "I reminded them of my other responsibilities, and they offered to help me prioritize my work. But I know what that really means. Instead of fifty-hour work weeks, I'll be here until ten o'clock every night and many Saturdays."

Ben looked concerned, and it hit me that I sounded like I was whining. He asked me about what had gone wrong with my initial presentation to Andrew, and I explained.

Ben took notes throughout my introduction and appeared to smirk a bit when I explained the outcomes of my research and the plan template I had handed to Andrew. Once I was done with my summary, Ben put his pen down, looked up, and started by sharing relevant background about Felder.

"When I joined Felder, I was surprised that we hadn't begun work on planning for a disruption. And I'm equally surprised that none of our customers has pushed us to address this specific risk before now. We have serious vulnerabilities.

"In the last calendar year, Felder manufactured twenty-nine different prescription pharmaceutical products for eighteen different global customers. The products produced by Felder are often produced at only one manufacturing location. Each of its products is 'validated' by the FDA or another country's equivalent regulatory agency. This regulatory validation requires rigid supply chain, production, and quality processes executed to exacting standards. Each customer is required to seek regulatory approval to market and sell these products. Therefore, Felder is unable to change or move production processes unless granted approval by the regulatory agency and the customer. Of the twenty-nine different products, Felder is the sole-source manufacturer for fifteen of them.

"As you know, in addition to our headquarters in Cleveland, Ohio, Felder has a total of seven manufacturing locations around the world. Each site holds raw materials and warehouses of finished goods onsite until the product is shipped to the customer or a distributor. Felder does not maintain a centralized distribution center in any of its markets.

"Felder has a complex supply chain littered with single and sole-source providers. Over the years, decisions made to engage with a single provider for a product were made primarily for financial reasons, although in some cases, only one provider is available to supply a product."

I couldn't help but be amazed as to how much Ben knew about Felder.

He continued, "Three years ago, Felder made the decision to implement SAP for many of its financial and operational processes. The SAP environment, together with many of the internal systems, runs in the cloud. Felder also employs numerous software as a service (SaaS) applications. Nearly all its 'noncloud' and non-SaaS systems are physically in one third-party data center in Virginia, although its VOIP phone system is architected to be redundant across three sites (the Virginia data center, the Cleveland headquarters, and Concord).

"During a recent meeting with our account management team, I learned that two of our largest customers are making inquiries about business continuity. These inquiries are coming through the sales organization, and it's taken some time for them to catch senior management's attention, even though in one case we might be in breach of contract. As you know, the potential for getting the Paulsen account was the impetus needed to make a serious effort in this area.

And as you've learned, business continuity is far more than just a document. It's a significant and ongoing undertaking."

I picked up my pen to take a few notes as Ben continued.

"I think Paulsen is astute in suggesting, even mandating, that its most critical suppliers seek conformance to ISO 22301. But more on that later. First, I'm happy to provide some coaching and advice as you work on building the program. I just need to be honest, in that I can't spend a huge amount of my time on this right now, as I have two large projects plus my 'day job' to tackle."

With a frown, Ben told me that having a 'day job' plus extra projects is the Felder way. I frowned as well.

Ben continued, "At the same time, business continuity is something I'm passionate about, Michael, and I can tell you, I have lots of lessons learned to share. May I share a few things now, and maybe we can reconnect tomorrow to have some more time together?"

I nodded, and Ben continued, "Like you, when I first got involved in business continuity, I thought the outcome was a plan document, but it's so much more. It's about trying to minimize the frequency of a disruption by designing the business appropriately, affecting the culture of the organization, and getting its leaders to continually think about business continuity when making strategic decisions. But it's also about planning to enable recovery if any key resources become unavailable, such as people, buildings, equipment, IT, or suppliers. Beyond making the mistake in thinking that business continuity is all about a plan, the other trap that many people fall into is thinking it's all about IT."

"Where was Ben last week?" I wondered to myself.

"But there are two other things that are important to note. First, you should absolutely think strategically. By this, I mean that you need to be thinking about the continuity of our most important products, services, and supporting business processes. In other words, think top-down. Obviously, you can't do this effectively without thoroughly knowing the company. One of the biggest mistakes business continuity professionals make is assuming they can do their job effectively without an intricate knowledge of the business. I can't overemphasize how important it is to thoroughly know the company."

My mind wandered for a moment. I think this is what Shannon was getting at during our mentoring conversation. I snapped my attention back to Ben as he continued, "Second, you must actively engage with our senior leadership team as a means of understanding what they value most and ensuring the program is aligned with Felder's business strategy. I know you've been employed by Felder for only a short time, and you may not know it's common here to staff key initiatives with cross-functional steering committees. I strongly recommend you charter such a steering committee."

I wrote furiously, until Ben suggested we schedule an hour together the next day to continue talking. Then he suggested I buy a copy of ISO 22301 and read it before our next meeting. He said, "We used ISO 22301 when I ran the program at Creden. It serves as a great framework to tackle the problem of business continuity and connect it to the strategy of our business. It also describes a process of driving continual improvement over time. Do you think you will have time to read it before we meet again? It's not that long."

For the third time, I nodded. In addition to thanking Ben profusely, I promised to set up a time to meet the following day.

As he stood up, Ben looked me squarely in the eyes and offered one last bit of advice, as well as a cryptic comment. "To do business continuity well, you will need to prioritize it and get behind it. But business continuity may surprise you. If you do things right, you will get to meet people and learn the business far faster than if you were simply working in insurance or in the quality department. This assignment should help you tackle your insurance and ERM assignments. But if I'm wrong, and you're still unhappy with the assignment in about a month, you might want to have another meeting with Andrew to discuss this problem. Business continuity is far too important for Felder to have someone leading it that doesn't want to lead it."

With that, he left, and I felt a little disappointed in myself that I had been so open with Ben in our first meeting. Perhaps I shouldn't have shared my disdain for the assignment.

As soon as I got back to my office, I logged into the ISO website and bought a copy of ISO 22301. At less than twenty pages, it was an easy read. I had some familiarity with management system concepts because I'd been part of an ISO 9001 quality management system, so the content seemed familiar too. And in reading ISO 22301, I could see what Ben was talking about, specifically the need to engage leadership and treat the planning process as a recurring effort. And now I could see what Paulsen was expecting of our program. It started with the products we manufactured for them and included the supporting business processes necessary to successfully ship these products on behalf of Paulsen to its customers.

After that initial meeting with Ben and then reading ISO 22301, I think I understood the big picture a little better, but I still struggled with how to get started, especially in a culture I didn't quite know. And my other concern remained: how I would do this and get my other work done? Although I was happy Ben was available to coach me, I was worried he'd try to influence me to produce a world-class program that required my full-time attention, and I wasn't sure how much I could expect from him. After all, the guy had his own job to do. Still, my second meeting with Ben couldn't come soon enough.

Chapter 6

Getting (Re)Started

After tossing and turning all night, I woke up the next day with a mixture of dread and excitement about tackling this assignment. The twinge of excitement was related to Ben's promise that I'd learn about Felder and get to know the management team.

Reading ISO 22301 had reinforced my new-found understanding of the need to get the organization to 'do' business continuity appropriately. That's what Ben had been getting at. In tackling the business continuity assignment, I would learn a lot about Felder and have incredible opportunities to engage with the leadership team. I needed to stop sulking because this assignment might be a huge win-win opportunity—assuming I did a good job. The only alternative was to struggle in front of the entire leadership team, leave Felder, and go back to consulting.

As I pulled into the parking lot that morning, I made a commitment to myself: I needed to go all-in on this project, at least for a few months anyway.

I got to the office at 7:30 a.m., long before my meeting with Ben at 11 a.m. We had decided to meet this time in my office. I blocked the first three hours of the day to prepare for the meeting by outlining an approach to design and implement Felder's business continuity program, based on yesterday's conversation and on what I'd read in the ISO 22301 standard.

First, I reviewed my notes from the initial meeting with Ben and then looked over the clauses I had highlighted in the print version of the ISO 22301 standard. I decided to establish a top ten list of next steps to design and implement our program:

1. Establish business continuity program roles and responsibilities, including a steering committee

2. Identify business continuity obligations, meaning expectations like those Paulsen had conveyed as a service-level agreement

3. Scope the program in terms of products, services, and business processes, and set objectives for the business continuity program based on the outcomes that the program should deliver

4. Develop and seek approval for business continuity requirements, such as downtime tolerances, resource needs, and even opportunities to decrease the likelihood of a disruption (ISO 22301 calls this a BIA and risk assessment)

5. Identify gaps in how well we've previously prepared based on the business continuity requirements we've identified, and determine strategies to close these gaps

6. Document plans to describe how we would respond to a disruption and how we would implement the recovery strategies

7. Train stakeholders on how to participate in the planning process and how to participate in the response and recovery process when we're in 'crisis mode'

8. Exercise and test business continuity strategies to see whether they work and/or identify ways to improve

9. Perform management reviews with the steering committee to present performance metrics and get input on prioritizing improvement opportunities

10. Drive continual improvement by addressing management's prioritized corrective actions

I then prepared to get Ben's feedback. Reviewing the list, I couldn't help but wince once again at the memory of Andrew's reaction to the hasty and inadequate template I had presented to him. At least I still had the opportunity to redeem myself. With Ben's feedback, I should be ready to create a project plan to describe timing, participation, and outcomes for Andrew's feedback next week.

Right on time, Ben arrived in my office. It turned out I wasn't the only one who had come prepared for the meeting. I started by thanking Ben again for his time and insight yesterday. I apologized for my attitude and shared with him my commitment to get this business continuity initiative to a good place. I let him know I had purchased a copy of and read ISO 22301, explained some of my background with ISO 9001, and introduced my top ten list.

Appearing to be genuinely impressed with my progress, and perhaps my revised attitude, Ben took some notes. He told me he agreed with the top ten list, the order of the proposed next steps, and the approach for my next meeting with Andrew.

Just when I thought we were about to end the meeting early because we were on the same page, he threw me a curveball.

"I can tell you're feeling good about your plan. Thirteen years ago, when I was assigned business continuity responsibility, I had no experience, and I found a mentor to get me started. I didn't have ISO 22301, but I had a distant relative of the standard, that being British Standard (BS) 25999-2. It was helpful. I found a lot of books to read, and my mentor ran a great program that provided a ton of insight. As a result, I came up with a top ten list similar to yours. And I ran with it!"

I stared at him, my eyes asking Ben to tell me what happened.

"To be honest," Ben continued, "it was a struggle. Progress was much slower than I anticipated. I felt like I constantly took three steps forward then two steps back. There were many spreadsheets—I did a huge BIA survey, and guess what I learned? Everybody thinks his or her area is critical. I tried to keep everyone happy, but it got harder and harder as time went on.

"Before I knew it, we were three years into the program, and I was ready to give up. I think I can say I honestly hated my job, probably in many ways like the way you felt yesterday!"

We both laughed, and then Ben continued, "I sat down with my boss to lay it all on the table. He helped me see what was going on, and he boiled it down to two core issues:

1. I was casting too wide a net: my program scope was too large, and everything was designated as critical.

2. People were dreading when I might call on them to participate in the planning process. In most cases, I struggled to get people, including our senior leadership team, to attend. People were bored with business continuity. In many ways, it was always the same thing during meetings: me talking and asking them to do things."

Ben must have seen me slump into my chair.

He smiled in a conciliatory manner. "Not to worry. The issues I experienced made me think about how to add value to the organization and make business continuity more interesting. For those first three years, I had gathered advice on *what* to do (like a BIA) or outcomes I should be working to achieve (like a plan), but I struggled with finding proven methods on *how* to do these things."

I didn't dare interrupt Ben, but I agreed. During my hours of internet searches, I found a lot on what to do, but not too much guidance on how to do it.

Ben continued, "I don't know what sparked it, but I got interested in solving two of the biggest problems I was facing. I ended up labeling them 'Focus' and 'Engagement.' The funny thing is, I soon discovered that most in the business continuity profession face the same challenge."

He paused, and I had to ask, "Did you eventually figure it out?"

He smiled again. "I think I made a lot of progress. In fact, in my last five years at Creden, I had the opportunity to present what I had learned at several industry conferences, and I'm confident my presentations had a positive effect on many organizations' levels of preparedness. Perhaps most important, I had a lot more fun—and I think the people who participated in my program had more fun too.

"I even named my approach—I called it the Business Continuity Operating System, or BCOS. BCOS provides the *how* that so many people seem to struggle with."

I made a note to do an internet search and look for any of Ben's recorded presentations.

Ben continued, "After we met yesterday, when I shared with you my time constraints, it hit me. I miss spreading the word about what I learned as a business continuity program manager. I miss sharing my approach. Talking about business continuity yesterday—for the first time in three years—relit that spark, and I wanted to mention that I am really excited about helping you get us to a good place."

I'm sure I did a bad job of hiding my excitement. I must have been beaming.

Ben gave me a scowl, pointed a finger in my direction and bellowed, "But I'm not going to do this for you!"

We both laughed again.

Before I knew it, our hour was up, and I hadn't yet learned much about the BCOS. Ben assured me again that he wasn't disappearing and suggested we meet again the following day so he could begin to connect what I learned through my ISO 22301 research to the BCOS model. Naturally, I agreed.

Before leaving my office, Ben suggested that I work on the project charter and project schedule to get the program designed and implemented based on the top ten list. From there, we could weave in the BCOS model. We also briefly discussed the difference between a business continuity project and the business continuity program. Ben and I agreed that my goal was to develop a project plan that addressed the design and implementation of the business continuity program in Year One, while not losing sight of the need to build the program for long-term success. To him, that was the difference between a project and a program—and I agreed.

Chapter 7

Introducing BCOS

I spent the remainder of the afternoon working to meet the commitment I had made to Ben, to create my first draft of the project charter. I resurrected my old Project Management Institute (PMI) training materials and crafted a document that succinctly described the problem, the desired outcome, roles/responsibilities, timing, and approach. As Ben suggested, my approach documented in the project charter aligned to my top ten list. I remembered that Ben had reminded me that Felder's first year of business continuity will closely resemble a project but will quickly transition to a program comprised of repeated processes and tasks.

Feeling good about my progress, and a lot more at ease now that I knew Ben was motivated to help, I spent the last hour of the day returning to my 'day job.' During my 4:30 p.m. call with our insurance broker, Kyle Thomas, I discussed my new assignment with him.

I was surprised that he was very interested in my work on business continuity and wanted me to keep him informed regarding my progress. He told me that he works with many of his clients on the outcomes of their business continuity processes to better understand financial exposure, as well as maximum downtime potential. He had some success using this information with the major carriers to seek premium reductions, given that the carriers' risk is both known and controlled. Before discussing the current renewal, I added Kyle as a new, key stakeholder in my project charter.

Following my one-hour call with Kyle, I went home early for the first time in over a week, secretly looking forward to my meeting with Ben at 9 a.m. the next morning.

He arrived on time the next day and handed me a piece of paper. Ben started, "Well, I didn't have too much time yesterday to dig up all of my old business continuity materials, but I did find a one-page summary of how I've previously implemented the BCOS model I mentioned to you yesterday. Just to be clear, this wasn't how I did it at first at Creden Corporation. Based on my lessons learned there, and some work I did later as a consultant for other organizations, this is the approach I turned into what I call my 'proven process.'"

He continued, "I don't want to make this bigger than it is. As you can see, I eventually summarized my approach to implement a business continuity program using the BCOS model using six iterative processes. I called these processes Startup, Analysis, Strategy, Plans, Exercise, and Improve. It's important to note that Analysis through Exercise is very closely aligned to the methodology that you read about in ISO 22301. At times I chose to execute the ISO 22301 methodology creatively.

"I will share how I did that—but Analysis through Exercise isn't the special part. And just to connect the dots between our conversations yesterday and now, your top ten list that you shared with me yesterday is very much aligned to Analysis through Exercise. As we work together, you'll see that the Startup process, glossed over by most, is essential. When you get the Startup process right, the other processes have the greatest chance of success."

I was staring at the white piece of paper with six gray boxes.

"So, this is it? This is what I need to do to get business continuity right here at Felder?" I asked.

Ben quickly responded with a nod. "At a summary level, that's it. We do need to go a little deeper on a few things, but we can do so over time as you work through your project plan."

Ben continued, "As a first step in Startup, if we can get the program sponsor's attention, and that of other senior leaders, to engage in an open conversation on four Frame Questions, we will have the input you need to deliver a focused, Year-One business continuity program."

Ben went to my dry-erase board and wrote four questions:

1. Why are we doing business continuity?
2. What are we trying to protect?
3. How much business continuity do we need?
4. Who should be involved in the program?

The questions made sense to me. Well, except for the third one. But nonetheless, I nodded.

"Michael, my recommendation to you is to approach next week's meeting with Andrew as a blend of project introduction and a Frame Meeting. Get his input and feedback and ask whether he feels it's appropriate to bring in the other members of the leadership team to offer their input to ensure everyone is on the same page as to what business continuity means to Felder. I doubt Andrew will want to be the only member of the senior leadership team to offer input on the program design."

I had known Andrew only for a few months, but based on my understanding of Felder's collaborative culture, I agreed he would want a larger meeting.

"One more thing, Michael. Remember when I mentioned to you that, at a summary level, BCOS is essentially six straightforward *processes*? That's true—but there are seven *ingredients* that must be present for this to work. I want to explain them to you, and then I'll have given you enough for today. It should be enough for you to prepare for next Friday's meeting with Andrew."

I agreed, and he continued, "For the BCOS to work, the business continuity program manager needs to use sound business practices to engage and create meaningfulness for everyone involved and be strategic when tackling the problem of preparedness. There are seven ingredients, or truths, that enable the BCOS to work over the long term, and I think I proved that at Creden. I understand the program remains a model of effectiveness today, and management is highly confident that their program provides the right level of resilience."

Leaving the white piece of paper aside this time, Ben walked up to my dry-erase board again, erased the four Frame Questions, and wrote:

1. Frame

2. Process

3. Participation

4. Engagement

5. Measurables

6. Improvement

7. Automation

"These are the ingredients and what makes BCOS special. I am confident that if a business continuity program manager focuses on these seven things when operating a business continuity program, he or she will achieve a strategic connection to the organization, engage the right people appropriately, and achieve the meaningful goal for all program participants in a pragmatic manner."

I looked over the list. Again, before I could start asking questions, Ben seemed to read my mind and began explaining, "Yes, Frame is a BCOS process step, but I also consider it an ingredient for success. The key here is that the executive management team and all other program participants are in complete agreement regarding the answers to the four Frame Questions, and they use that information to tackle the problem of business continuity risk. I don't think it makes sense to cover all seven BCOS ingredients right now. We can do so over the next few months."

I nodded.

In watching Ben talk about BCOS and its ingredients, I could see his passion. When I first met him, I saw him as a guy who rarely gets out of a quality lab—kind of reserved and unexcitable. My impression was the opposite now, and quite frankly, I found Ben's excitement contagious.

"Ben, this makes sense, and it's really interesting how you took years of trial and error with business continuity to develop the BCOS. And I thought business continuity was a little stuffy and a one-and-done thing that's all about creating plans!"

We both laughed, and then I continued, "You mentioned that we can pause on some of these ingredients and instead focus on preparation for the meeting with Andrew next Friday. I assume we need to focus on presenting the recommended process and prepare to get his input on the four Frame Questions?"

He answered with one word: "Precisely."

And with that, he packed up his things and left.

After our meeting on Friday, Ben emailed me some materials he'd found regarding his BCOS model. He shared a number of files, which included a presentation that he gave at a *Disaster Recovery Journal* conference six years ago, a sample Frame Meeting presentation he created about seven years ago, a policy statement template (that he must have created for Creden), and some additional process documentation that he called a "program standard operating procedure (SOP)." I looked it over before I ended the day and closed my laptop, and then my wife and I headed off for the weekend to an out-of-town wedding. My plan was to dive into preparing for my meeting with Andrew first thing Monday morning.

Chapter 8

It's Not All About Methodology

I must admit, I didn't give much thought to work after I packed up on Friday at 5 p.m. It was a great weekend, and I came back to work refreshed, feeling personally challenged to knock it out of the park with Andrew on Friday. I blocked my calendar 100 percent through Wednesday to make sure I'd be fully prepared for the meeting.

I started my Monday by looking at the presentation that Ben had given about six years ago. It was so different from the multitude of presentations I had found by searching the topic of business continuity. Instead of a presentation on how to perform a BIA, what needed to be in a plan, how to facilitate an exercise, and blah blah blah, Ben's presentation was all about leadership, employee engagement, and creating a program that was meaningful for everyone involved.

Around slide ten or eleven, Ben introduced the approach he'd used to get the program going at Creden and drive improvement. It included the same six steps he'd listed on the paper he had left with me last week.

STARTUP ▶ ANALYSIS ▶ STRATEGY ▶ PLANS ▶ EXERCISE ▶ IMPROVE

He also presented what he called the 'essential ingredients' for business continuity success. This time, instead of a list, it was a wheel diagram.

I studied each of the elements and realized that, other than Frame, which Ben had explained to me on Friday, I needed a lot more context before I could understand what Ben had in mind with the other ingredients. Then I remembered he'd told me that he'd explain the others over time as we worked through the project.

The rest of the presentation included a more in-depth explanation of Startup through Improve. Naturally, because of the meeting with Andrew on Friday, I focused on the Frame-related content. After flipping through the five slides that covered Frame, it hit me that this concept was very straightforward, perhaps too straightforward. But I could see how it would be necessary to connect the business continuity program to Felder's overall business strategy.

My biggest takeaway from reviewing the presentation was that if I covered the four high-level questions with Andrew—and with the executive leadership team—I would get the input necessary to design a program that met Felder's needs. Ben's presentation highlighted almost the same four questions he had written on my dry-erase board:

1. Why is business continuity important to this business?
2. What are we trying to protect?
3. How much business continuity do we need?
4. Who should sponsor, lead, and participate in the program?

It would be great to hear Ben facilitate this conversation for real, but I knew that wouldn't be possible before the end of the week. I made a note to ask him to give me some sample outcomes of this conversation.

Next, I opened the sample Frame Meeting presentation Ben had given me on Friday. It aligned with the presentation he had given at the conference, but it also included some background information on business continuity. The presentation also included information on his approach to reimplement the business continuity program at Creden. I figured this presentation would be a great structure for my meeting with Andrew on Friday—updated, of course, to reflect my project charter and the ten steps I outlined.

Still, I knew I needed more for this meeting. Specifically, I needed to give some thought to *how* I would answer each of the four Frame Questions, and the other five business continuity essential ingredients.

I closed my office door, powered up my laptop, and started to type.

Frame

I started with Frame and gave some thought as to how I would answer each of the four questions.

1. Why is business continuity important to this business?

I thought about how Andrew would answer this question. Beyond the obvious, that being Paulsen's requirement for a business continuity program,

I guessed that he and the rest of the executive team recognize that it's the right thing to do. It's a fiduciary responsibility to protect everyone's interests, including those of shareholders, employees, and even the patients using the products we manufacture.

To me, this question was a way to summarize expectations and obligations, meaning anything regulatory-related, as well as anything we promised our customers.

2. What are we trying to protect?

Felder does not own any of its patents or formularies for the products it produces for clinical trials and commercial purposes. Rather, its customers are the ones contracting with Felder to support them or manufacture the clinical or commercial therapies. Based on the services we offer, I imagined we would want to have business continuity capabilities in place for process development, administering adverse events reporting, clinical trials management processes, and, of course, manufacturing and distribution—regardless of location.

In thinking about this answer further, I began to wonder what conversations we'd had with our customers about manufacturing-related business continuity because, in our industry, we can't simply move production to another location without significant regulatory approvals and testing. And we'd have multiple production locations for all products only if the customer demanded it and was willing to pay for it. I made a note to ensure I brought this situation up to Andrew on Friday.

3. How much business continuity do we need?

I found the third Frame Question to be somewhat strange. I watched one of Ben's recorded presentations where he discussed the Frame Meeting, and I paid special attention to this part. He suggested that the facilitator be prepared to ask the meeting participants what they felt their downtime tolerance should be for the in-scope product and services, or for the major internal business processes that needed to be protected. During the presentation, Ben instructed the audience that a facilitator might also need to ask the participants what level of impact on the customer they were willing to accept or tolerate.

For our organization, my thoughts went straight to our long lead time of raw materials and manufacturing single points of failure. I assumed our customer and patient call centers were in one location, too, and might take some time to recover. I was very interested in Andrew's opinions because only he and the other members of the executive management team could truly answer those questions.

4. Who should sponsor, lead, and participate in the program?

This one seemed a little easier to me. I figured Andrew was the program sponsor, and I was the program manager or leader (only temporarily, I hoped). I hadn't thought much about other participants. I figured I would need input from other vice presidents and managers regarding their risks and resource needs, but at this point, that was just a guess.

Based on my review of Ben's materials and after thinking through the Frame Questions, I started to become more at ease. That combined with Ben's endorsement of my project charter!

After listening to a recorded webinar that Ben gave on all seven of the BCOS ingredients, I continued thinking about how they applied to Felder.

Process

Ben had written some notes under the Process ingredient, namely, 'documented' and 'followed by all.' When Ben had talked about Process during his webinar, he'd mentioned the need for business continuity management process documentation, something that program participants could review to explain how to meet expectations. He mentioned that process documentation should be written for everyone in the organization. He also mentioned that it needed to be socialized so everyone was aware process documentation existed, *and* program participants needed to be held accountable to follow it consistently. It was that latter point that described what he meant by 'followed by all.'

Again, I made a note to request some examples from Ben, as he mentioned that one form of process documentation is a policy statement and another is a set of SOPs.

Participation

The third essential ingredient had a bit of overlap with one of the Frame Questions. Again, I felt it was safe to assume that I had been assigned the role of project manager and, possibly, also that of the interim business continuity program manager. Because I report to Andrew, I assumed that Andrew was the executive program sponsor. I could request that he chair the future steering committee that Ben suggested I charter.

Regarding the steering committee, I thought about this some more. I have formed and participated in risk management–related steering committees in the past, and I've always found that smaller is better. But I needed to make sure that this steering committee reflected the scope of the future-state program. Given my thoughts on the Frame Meeting response to the 'what are we trying to protect' question, I intended to recommend to Andrew that the steering committee membership include seven roles (Andrew and six others):

- COO – Shannon Carter
- CIO – Anne Shoemaker
- SVP, Business Development – Steve Henry
- SVP, General Counsel – Jacob Cunningham
- VP, Human Resources – Jack Tanner
- VP, Strategic Services – Melissa Zak

The last role I noted in the project charter was that of business process owner. Having been with Felder for only nine weeks, I still knew very little about the company's operations. According to Ben, even if I had been employed by Felder for thirty years, he recommended I design a decentralized program that ensured business process owners were actively engaged in the business continuity process in a recurring manner. So I noted the business process owner as a key role, but

I didn't know which business process owners needed to be engaged just yet. I wouldn't know that until I confirmed the program scope with Andrew.

Engagement

Again, I hit the play button on Ben's recorded webinar. Building on the decisions made regarding Participation, Ben recommended establishing a regular cadence of interactions with the different stakeholder groups. He mentioned that, early in the program, the project manager might need to meet with the steering committee and business process owners more frequently than in Year Two and beyond.

In his webinar, Ben mentioned that if there is a centralized team of business continuity experts that focuses exclusively on business continuity, they should meet weekly for what's called the Focus Meeting. He also discussed a specific, repeating agenda to get them focused on which parts of the organization to help. He mentioned three other meeting types too.

Ben's model for engagement seemed to be overkill. Was he really asking me to schedule forty-three meetings each year? Andrew would be irate if I requested that level of business involvement! I made a commitment to push back on this requirement.

Specific to the project work I needed to tackle, I figured that my initial request for meetings would be:

- Andrew and the steering committee: monthly for an hour until we completed the third project milestone, and then determine how often to meet

- Business process owners: based on specific project tasks, plus quarterly meetings to share what is working, ask questions, and review program measurables

Measurables

I understood the concept of measurables, especially given my Six Sigma training and the mantra, "what gets measured gets done." But I wasn't sure what business continuity measurables looked like. Again, I hit the play button on Ben's webinar.

Ben mentioned two types of measurables that resonate with different stakeholder groups:

1. Product/service measurables

2. Activity and compliance measurables

He described product/service measurables as the ability to meet product/service-related downtime tolerances. In our case, I assumed that two example product/service metrics could be taking an adverse event report from a patient or being able to manufacture a product. Ben indicated that some organizations call these key risk indicators, or KRIs.

He described activity and compliance measurables as reporting whether the organization and its program participants were doing the planning work they needed, as described in process documentation. He said some organizations call these key performance indicators, or KPIs.

Overall, in thinking about the topic of measurables, I didn't think I would be in a position to define them until after I'd had the Frame Meeting and had approved process documentation.

Improvement

The next essential ingredient was Improvement. I hit play again.

Ben mentioned three forms of Improvement that are essential to drive progress, stay relevant to the organization's strategy, and ensure expectations are met.

1. Goals

2. Actions

3. Experiments

In the webinar, Ben suggested establishing quarterly goals endorsed by the steering committee, as well as one- and three-year strategic goals to drive an appropriate level of resiliency. He mentioned that this approach is useful in defining business continuity as enduring in nature, not one-and-done in a year.

Ben described actions—such as ISO 22301 corrective actions—as necessary to solve performance problems or address failures to meet a requirement or expectation. He said it is best to solve root causes and ensure owners are assigned to drive actions to closure. He also had success in reviewing and getting the steering committee to prioritize and endorse high-priority or critical actions and asking each member to sponsor one of the most important actions.

The concept of improving experiments was interesting to me. My first thought was that it was cheesy or, at best, a fad. Ben advocated the use of experiments to drive ownership and engagement throughout the organization. He considered experiments a form of actions, but the idea was to get different program participants to come up with an idea and try it out—often failing but learning from the failure to drive continual improvement. Ben lit up during the webinar when he was talking about experiments because he believed that this aspect of Improvement drove employee engagement and a sense of ownership.

I added this to my list of pushback items for a future conversation with Ben.

Automation

The last essential ingredient was Automation. Before this, I hadn't realized that software focused on improving business continuity outcomes even existed.

Ben commented that most leading organizations are highly complex, with considerable resources and interdependencies combining to deliver products and services. He went on to explain that with ongoing organizational and environmental change, as well as inherent complexity, software that digitized the organization was essential to do the following:

1. Identify vulnerabilities, or what he called the hidden cracks

2. Determine appropriate business continuity requirements

3. Understand each 'critical path' to deliver products and services

4. Identify the implications, or 'what if,' when a disruption affects one or more activities and resources

In his presentation, he summarized that the Automation value proposition centered on automating manual tasks, delivering intelligence to drive decision-making, and integrating with other risk management solutions.

I made a note to do some more research in this area.

Chapter 9

Prepping for 'Andrew Part II'

After thinking about the 'essential ingredients,' I felt pretty good about continuing my work on the project charter that I'd begun last week. If my approach covered each of the ingredients and the management system–related best practices summarized in ISO 22301, I felt I would be on the right track.

With my preliminary thoughts on how the essential ingredients applied to Felder, the input provided by Ben, the ISO 22301 content, and my top ten list that Ben had endorsed, I started to write. I began by describing the different project activities and outcomes.

I felt good about the activities (partially because I had cheated a bit and consulted a sample project plan Ben gave me), but timing was my big unknown. Time estimation was tough, especially since I didn't know which parts of the business would be in scope or how long tasks typically take (or how Felder's senior leadership team makes strategic decisions). With these unknowns in mind, I took a conservative approach and included high-level timing for my three major project milestones:

1. **Milestone #1: Design the business continuity program consistent with ISO 22301** (two months)

   - Establish business continuity program roles and responsibilities, including a steering committee (outcome: charter and monthly project updates)

- Conduct a Frame Meeting to identify business continuity expectations, scope the program, and set objectives (outcome: business continuity policy and SOPs)

2. **Milestone #2: Perform the first cycle of the business continuity process for Felder** (seven months)

   - Develop and seek approval for business continuity requirements (BIA and risk assessment)

   - Identify gaps in preparedness and determine strategies to close these gaps

   - Document plans

   - Train stakeholders

   - Exercise and test business continuity strategies

3. **Milestone #3: Get the organization started on Improve** (three months)

   - Perform management reviews with the steering committee and present performance metrics

   - Drive continual improvement through prioritized corrective actions

Another unknown was the need for resources. During my online research, I came across numerous consultancies and software providers, but I wasn't sure whether we needed either to be successful. In my project charter, I noted a possible future need that was currently undefined.

Next, I thought about the communication needs for a few stakeholders:

1. Senior leadership team, including Andrew

2. In-scope business process owners

3. Support functions, including facilities, human resources, procurement, IT, and compliance

4. Internal audit

5. Our board of directors

6. Our customers, including Paulsen

7. Our suppliers

Depending on the task or the need for an update, feedback, or approval, I needed to not only plan *when* to communicate but also the *best way* to engage each group. I essentially created a matrix by project task, who I needed to engage, and how. I could figure out timing when I created the project schedule.

Ben suggested creating an engagement plan after the Frame Meeting so that once I confirmed program participants and stakeholders, I would remain organized with engagement and communications. I made a note to get more information from Ben on what he meant by engagement plan and ask whether he had an example.

The last section of my draft project charter addressed quality measures and how our project team would ensure high-quality, strategy-aligned business continuity outcomes. I inferred, based on my conversations with Ben, that I could count on the steering committee and business process owners, but maybe I could rely on our internal audit department for an independent review as well.

With that said, I wrapped up my first draft of the project charter in about a day and a half. I emailed it and my first draft of the Frame Meeting presentation to Ben and asked for a review prior to our meeting on Wednesday. In parallel, I logged into Smartsheet, Felder's project scheduling tool, and started creating tasks, assignments, and timing based on the twelve-month milestone schedule summarized in my project charter. I figured I would show that to Ben when we met on Wednesday as well.

One thing I had learned was that Ben's coaching style is very developmental, meaning he likes to ask questions to steer me toward what he thinks is the right answer (based on his experiences). On Wednesday, Ben didn't disappoint. He clearly came prepared to our meeting and launched into a series of questions to help expand or refine my project charter.

He started off with the obligatory deadpan comment (that sounded a little like paternal pride), "I looked at the Frame deck and project charter . . . not bad at all."

And then he continued, "I reviewed the project charter end to end, and I think this is a great start. I have no doubt Andrew will be impressed. But let me ask a few questions.

"First, I imagine you'll run into roadblocks as you engage the business when rolling out the business continuity program. Besides Andrew, who we know will be busy, any thoughts on a key business ally to effect change?"

I could see that one key project role would be internal audit, so I would need to ask for their review at key milestones.

Next, Ben asked, "Another thought I had when reviewing the project charter had to do with some of the supporting roles throughout the business, mainly resource owners or subject matter experts who might help assess risk or determine business continuity strategies. Any thoughts there?"

Beyond my immediate response, IT, I could see where he was heading. It would be great to get a sense of business continuity-related controls and gaps from facilities, human resources, and procurement. Instantly, I had three more roles for my project charter. I wrote them in the margin of my printed copy of the project charter.

"What do you think about employee engagement, especially with rolling out expectations and knowledge of your future-state plans? Should they be a stakeholder?"

Another great point. In addition to customers (another stakeholder group I hadn't paid enough attention to), I didn't talk about the effect the project outcomes would have on our employees.

"One of my key lessons learned ten years ago had to do with organizational roadblocks. I don't mean just people who are difficult to work with. I mean key stakeholders that might slow you down but for the right reasons. They could be invaluable in helping you to avoid project landmines. Any thoughts here?"

I was honestly stumped, as I wasn't sure where Ben was going with this question. I shrugged, and he continued, "We operate in a highly regulated environment. Internally, we must have compliance's backing and, externally, the approval of FDA regulators. Collectively, we need their buy-in, or our steering committee will be unlikely to move forward, and our customers won't either."

Another great addition to both project roles/responsibilities and key stakeholders.

Ben endorsed the project activities I proposed and concurred with my assessment that the timing would be heavily influenced by the steering committee's input on scope.

We ended our meeting with Ben's promise to send me some additional project charter notes by noon Thursday.

The remainder of my Wednesday and all of Thursday were filled with reading and digging a little deeper into various articles and presentations that I found on the internet. I did a few LinkedIn searches for those with business continuity–related titles in pharmaceutical and biotech and made a few connections. I figured I would need some additional perspectives as we moved forward in the program design and execution.

By close of business on Thursday, I felt confident that I was far more prepared for my meeting with Andrew than I had been last time. I emailed him a copy of the Frame Meeting presentation and the project charter at 4 p.m. with a request for a high-level review prior to our meeting.

The next morning, I rode the elevator to the tenth floor to Andrew's office. His door was open. I knocked, and he motioned me in. Unlike the stern look on his face last week, he smiled when greeting me.

Holding up a copy of the presentation, Andrew said, "This is a monumental improvement. I think this aligns with what Corey and Paulsen will be expecting. I really don't have any feedback at this point."

Then he smiled and asked, "This whole effort is a lot more than a plan, isn't it?" I sheepishly smiled and nodded. "Just a little."

Andrew continued, "So what's next? What do you need from me?"

I began, "As I was preparing for our meeting today, I was originally planning to guide you through the Frame Meeting materials to get answers to my four questions. And then it hit me. You're probably going to want me to get input from many of your peers before proceeding."

He nodded. "Sure, set up one-on-one meetings with the team. Do you want to talk through these questions with me now?"

I took a deep breath. "Well, at first I wanted to get only your input on this, as I thought you would be the best person to provide answers. Ben coached me that I probably need to get everyone's input on this."

Andrew interrupted, "Right, let's go through this and then you can set up the meetings with people like Shannon." He seemed a little annoyed.

This time I interrupted, "But Ben strongly suggested I get the executive team together at the same time to discuss the four Frame Questions. He helped me see that I need the team's collective input."

Andrew looked visibly concerned. "Impossible. Do you have any idea how hard it is to get them together? I have a standing meeting, but we have packed agendas as it is. You're asking for sixty to ninety minutes to cover this with all of them?"

Ben had warned me that Andrew might resist, and I was ready, or I thought I was. "Andrew, I need the executive team together so everyone is on the same page, and so that all participants can benefit from hearing one another respond.

The value is in the debate. Ben warned me, and I agree, that failing to take this approach could result in a lot of rework and missed executive management expectations. His experience also taught him that activities such as the BIA are much harder without an executive team on the same page regarding scope and downtime tolerance."

I took a deep breath and made one more point, "If business continuity is as important as you, Sara, and Corey think it is, I don't think we can afford *not* to do this."

Andrew looked up and gave me a fake smile. "Well played. Okay, I support your recommendation. You're right; I wouldn't want to solely influence the foundation of our business continuity program. A cross-functional discussion with members of our senior leadership team could be valuable."

He continued, "I advise you to not only prepare to ask those four questions but also have an idea of how you would respond. Don't walk into a meeting with this group with a blank sheet of paper. Be prepared with your ideas and don't be afraid to push back and call BS. They are far more effective reacting to ideas than coming up with their own. Also, summarize Paulsen's requirements, a little about ISO 22301, your expectations of their roles, and those of their people. Lastly, make sure you have a good understanding of our core business processes."

And then he simply asked, "Does that work?"

I then asked Andrew whether he agreed with my recommendation regarding the steering committee and the proposed participation.

He nodded.

With that, I thanked my boss for his time and counsel and promised a draft email that he could send to the members of the steering committee.

Before I left, Andrew told me I could have sixty to ninety minutes with the proposed steering committee the following Wednesday, continuing a meeting that he had already scheduled.

As I was walking out of Andrew's office, I asked one more question, "Can I ask Sara Terrence from internal audit to review the project charter and observe our meetings with the steering committee? It might be good to have an independent perspective as we execute this program design and the implementation effort."

"That's a great idea. Set up some time with Sara to introduce the project, and indicate I requested her involvement. By the way, I forgot to ask, has Ben been helpful? I'm guessing that's a stupid question because you seemed well prepared for this meeting."

I smiled again. "He's been invaluable."

Chapter 10

The Dry Run and Final Preparations

Andrew delivered. He got the recommended steering committee participants scheduled for a ninety-minute meeting six days later. I got the meeting invitation from his assistant forty minutes after I left his office.

I got straight to work, addressing exactly what Andrew suggested. I opened the draft Frame presentation I had shared with Andrew and made some edits.

1. I added a slide or two about ISO 22301.

2. I summarized Paulsen's request of us as part of question #1 (drivers).

3. Immediately preceding question #4 (participation), I did my best to describe some of the key program roles I envisioned, based on Ben's input and my research.

One bit of advice Andrew gave was trickier. He wanted to make sure I had a good understanding of our core processes coming into the Frame Meeting. I recalled the conversation I had with Ben about question #2, 'what are we trying to protect.'

He and I discussed some of Felder's core services and supporting business activities, namely, process development, administering adverse events reporting, clinical trials management, and, of course, manufacturing and distribution. I figured it was in my best interest to schedule a thirty-minute meeting with a director-level representative in each of those areas between now and Thursday, just to get a better sense of what was involved in each. To be honest, I was a little embarrassed that I didn't already know much about each of these areas, especially process development.

I also did one more thing: I scheduled a two-hour meeting with Ben for Tuesday, with the request that he play my role and facilitate a Frame Meeting using my materials. He happily agreed.

Tuesday afternoon's dry run with Ben arrived before I knew it, probably because I spent nearly all day Monday and half of Tuesday in a series of thirty-minute meetings getting to know Felder.

I booked a conference room on the third floor, plugged in my laptop, and opened the latest version of the presentation I had amended following the meeting with Andrew.

I told Ben that Andrew fully endorsed our approach and had scheduled the meeting for the day after tomorrow. I summarized the changes I made to the Frame presentation and my meetings with the different process owners throughout Felder.

"That's the best part of the job, Michael—getting to know how the organization works and how all the pieces come together to deliver value for our customers." Ben continued, "And your new-found knowledge will not only help with business continuity, but it will also help you connect the dots for your broader risk management objectives and make you an invaluable source of knowledge for others throughout the organization."

I certainly couldn't disagree with him. I had the thought that a summary of my experiences over the last forty-eight hours would be a great Felder orientation program for anyone joining the company.

Ben turned to the laptop, turned on presentation mode, and then looked over at me.

"How about if I play your role, Michael, and you play the role of every member of the steering committee? And one more idea. Should we record this meeting so you can play it back, if you'd like?"

I nodded, and Ben began. For the next two hours, Ben played the role of Frame Meeting facilitator and often paused to provide me with background information on why he presented the way he did.

Visit **castellanbc.com/felder** to listen to the dry run of the Frame Meeting, where Ben coaches Michael on how best to facilitate the meeting.

I liked that Ben presented in a way that included education, engaging me as the steering committee by asking good, probing questions. But because I was a fake steering committee, I often answered Ben's questions poorly, and he didn't hesitate to either clarify the question by asking it in a different way or explain what he was looking for. He also wasn't afraid to let awkward silence set in as I thought of an appropriate response. (I figured I would need to get comfortable with that!)

The dry run served as a great test of what I thought I had learned through my engagement with Andrew and the process owners. I took a few notes on where I needed to go back and ask some follow-up questions. It was clear Ben knew our business, and I could see how that helped him facilitate.

"Okay, that's the Frame Meeting," Ben concluded. "What do you think?"

"I don't know. It seems simple, maybe even too simple. And if this is one of the most important things to help me set the foundation for successful business continuity, this almost feels too easy. Also, with my limited experience, thinking quickly on my feet may be tough if they push back, and I'm not sure what I should ask to really probe and get the conversation going. It's obvious you know our business, and you've done this a million times."

Ben countered, "I can see your point. Remember when we first met and I shared that I had two to three years of lessons learned, and most were around focus and engagement? Remember when I mentioned that everything at Creden seemed critical? I overcame that with the second and third questions: 'what are we trying to protect' and 'how much business continuity do we need.' And remember when I mentioned diminishing program energy over time? That was the fourth question: 'who should sponsor, lead, and participate in the program.' I designed the Frame process to enable discussion, and the four questions—as well as the order of the four questions— to generate discussion."

I could see where he was coming from, but I still was skeptical. I just didn't say it.

Ben continued, "One more thing. Just remember, you're in a room among people that want you to succeed. And better yet, remember that this isn't your only shot at getting their guidance. Just relax, listen to this recording one more time, and however you prepare for presentations, do it."

With that, Ben got up, asked me to call him after the meeting on Thursday to let him know how it went, and left.

On Wednesday, I did exactly as Ben suggested. I listened to the recording one more time, ran through the presentation one more time (jotting down some ideas on probing questions), and had a few five-minute meetings with different process owners to get answers to my final questions.

Chapter 11

The Frame Meeting

The Journey – Status and Time Check

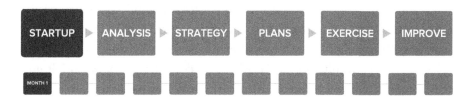

I couldn't wait to call Ben to summarize this afternoon's Frame Meeting. I don't think I was back in my office for more than ten seconds before I dialed his office number. I may have even been out of breath when Ben answered.

"Hello, this is Ben Campbell," came the voice on the other end of the phone.

I summarized the meeting, adding that not only did I think it was a success but I had also learned a lot from the meeting participants. In fact, the entire steering committee told me the meeting was time well spent. I also shared with Ben that the meeting had included some fireworks, with one member of the steering committee pushing back on the idea of having a high-level meeting such as this, and others debating whether we should be working on manufacturing business continuity capabilities or mandating that our client base pay for such capabilities.

I could almost picture Ben smiling, particularly as I shared the engaging meeting feedback provided by our COO, Shannon Carter.

"'I can't tell you how many times I've heard the same feedback, Michael,' she'd said. "When you create an atmosphere where people can work through problems by sharing their perspectives, great things happen.'"

"I assume you could sense a higher-than-normal energy level in the room when compared to other meetings you've participated in?" Ben asked.

"Without a doubt," I replied. "I also took your advice about encouraging the participants to openly share their thoughts and debate with one another. I reminded them that, absent their input, I wouldn't have the fuel to get the program going, let alone get it going in the right direction. I also mentioned that unless they were all on the same page, I would struggle with meeting seven different sets of expectations. And I used one of your very specific recommendations: as facilitator, I asked questions directly of those who seemed used to multitasking in these types of meetings, as well as those who seemed apprehensive about offering input. Melissa Zak of strategic services fell into that category, and as it turned out, she probably had the best sense of what our customers expect of us."

"Michael, you mentioned you learned a lot about the organization. Do you mind summarizing what came out as a result of the four questions?"

I pulled out my notes just to make sure I didn't miss anything. I started with the first question, 'why is business continuity important to us.'

"As expected, Andrew immediately pointed out that the catalyst for the start of the business continuity program was the request made by Paulsen. But he, as well as Shannon, immediately pointed out to the group that the need goes far beyond one client's requirement."

I said, "The group talked a lot about how the therapies being manufactured by Felder on behalf of its contract manufacturing customers literally save lives or, at a minimum, make patients' lives substantially better. In some cases, these drugs are one of a kind in treating rare diseases, and without them, some patients could die within weeks or months.

"I found it interesting that one member of the steering committee, Jacob, even admitted that he hadn't thought of Felder's responsibility that way, and he had essentially placed the burden on our customers to worry about these issues. He also admitted that he would shift his thinking immediately. By the way, he was the same person who didn't want to have the meeting!"

I could almost picture Ben smiling when he asked, "What else, Michael?"

"Well, after discussing Paulsen and the therapies we're producing today, I asked the group to think about Felder's core purpose, and whether there was anything else that might be a driver for business continuity. Sure enough, Steve Henry started an interesting discussion on some of our noncommercial manufacturing processes and why they too are deserving of the steering committee's attention. He pointed out that three of our service businesses speed therapies to market, meaning that in the absence of our expertise in process development or clinical trials management, many patients' access to life-saving medications would be delayed. He also reminded the group that, if our ability to administer some of our clients' adverse events reporting processes were to fail, people's lives could be immediately placed in unnecessary danger. It was interesting, Ben. When the group members talked about the patient, they were all nodding and hanging on each other's words. It was a series of powerful discussions. The idea of asking about Felder's core purpose really paid off."

Ben pushed the conversation forward, "It sounds like that discussion became a springboard into the second question, 'what are we trying to protect.'"

"Right. I introduced the question and then shared what you explained to me two weeks ago: the best organizations, regardless of industry, take a top-down look at themselves and start by scoping based on their most important products and services then look at their most time-sensitive processes, activities, and resources that contribute to each.

"Shannon and Steve seemed to be the most engaged with this question. They commented that, in addition to commercial manufacturing for our twenty-nine FDA-approved products, other core in-scope products and services had to be precommercial manufacturing, clinical trials management, adverse events reporting management, and process development. They debated whether some of the regulatory advisory services should be addressed, but after some discussion, they felt the service was too small and not as time-sensitive as the rest, so it was left out of scope. They also removed three other internal processes from scope—marketing, business development, and internal audit—because they said we should focus on preserving our current business rather than growing it and trying to improve it as a crisis was unfolding."

Ben then asked, "Did they discuss scoping based on locations at all?"

"Yeah, we spent a few minutes on that. They agreed that in addition to our corporate processes in Cleveland, which is where much of the process development, clinical trials management, and adverse events reporting takes place, five out of the seven manufacturing locations—which also have precommercial labs— should be in scope:

- Independence, OH

- New Brunswick, NJ

- Concord, CA

- Carolina, Puerto Rico

- Cork, Ireland

"They agreed that Portland and Quincy could be addressed in the future, given that these locations are just coming online and will be addressing less critical products. One person, whom I don't want to name, called these products 'recreational drugs,' I think!"

I could hear Ben laugh.

I continued, "When we discussed locations, Jacob raised the issue of clients paying for manufacturing business continuity versus getting it for free. Shannon took the other side of the argument, making the case that it was our fiduciary responsibility to protect manufacturing capability for the benefit of the patient. It seemed like every person offered his or her perspective, and in the end, I think the leadership team was all on the same page in concluding that we need to work to make manufacturing processes as resilient as possible, but—based on product criticality—we need to encourage our clients to consider paying for multisite product manufacturing. We also agreed we needed to be more transparent in communicating what manufacturing business continuity means and what the client receives when engaging with us."

Once I recapped the issue processing specific to manufacturing business continuity, I continued, "I then asked whether there were strategic plans in place to enter any new markets or change the strategy that might affect what Felder intends to protect with business continuity. Andrew addressed this question. He mentioned that most won't change, but there are some possible acquisitions on the horizon that will likely change the scope a bit. I could tell he didn't want to get into specifics at this time since the information is sensitive.

"Before I could transition the group to question three, Steve Henry reminded the group of a topic covered in a previous discussion. He pointed out that, for manufacturing-related efforts, Felder is not obligated to have a secondary manufacturing location unless the customer contracts for it. That may not be the case for other, less capital-intensive processes. Therefore, part of the scope for business continuity must be improving business development communications on this topic. Once again, there was lots of nodding.

"It was funny, Ben. It's been a long time since I led a meeting where I struggled to keep things moving because the meeting participants were so active. I tried to transition to question three, but Shannon raised another good point. She pointed out that each manufacturing site holds raw materials, and each one stores finished product in warehouses onsite until the product is shipped to the customer or a distributor. Felder does not maintain a centralized distribution center in any of its markets. To make matters worse, Felder has a complex supply chain, employing numerous single- and sole-source providers. Over the years, decisions made to engage with a single provider for a product were made primarily for financial reasons. Although, in some cases, only one provider is available to supply a product. Shannon strongly suggested to the group that more attention needed to be paid to the supply chain. Again, there was lots of nodding."

"Did you ever make it to question three?" Ben sarcastically asked.

"I did. Shannon's last point on supply chain risk ended question number two, so I introduced question three, 'how much business continuity do we need.' As I suspected, I received inquisitive—maybe even skeptical—looks, so I explained further. On the white board, I wrote the product/service scope that the group had just endorsed. Next to that list, I made another:

- Never down
- Four hours
- One day
- Three days
- One week
- Two weeks
- One month
- Two months

"I explained to the group that I wanted them to assign one of these downtime tolerances for each of the in-scope products/services. I explained I only needed some directional guidance, and we would work to validate this guidance later in the planning process. They dove right in. After about twenty minutes of downtime tolerance arguments—some of them heated, based on a wide range of justifications, including revenue, profitability, product availability in the supply system, client obligations, and patient impact—we had our answers to question three:

- Commercial manufacturing: two weeks
- Precommercial manufacturing: one month
- Clinical trials management: three days
- Adverse events reporting management: four hours
- Process development: two weeks

"Perhaps it was to be expected that some members of the steering committee would advocate for their business areas rather than for the business as a whole. In those cases, they offered lower downtime tolerances, and people like Andrew and Sara seemed to offer counterarguments that led to more realistic downtime tolerances. Jacob seemed the most risk tolerant and tended to argue that, if there wasn't a contractual obligation, there wasn't a need to act. In the end, the group got on the same page."

Surprised that we had a list in twenty minutes, Ben concluded, "Not bad at all. Now I'm not fully keeping track here, but did you have enough time to get to question four?"

"I did, with about twelve minutes to spare. I asked the question, 'who should sponsor, lead, and participate in the program.' Of course, Andrew cracked a joke—something about having already broken the news to me that I'm the program manager and had I forgotten such an important detail.

"I assured him I had not but that I needed to identify a program sponsor, steering committee, and participation throughout the business. Andrew continued by reminding the group that Corey had asked him to take on the program sponsor role and he had agreed, but he also asked whether anyone disagreed with this assignment. Steve didn't disagree, but he expressed concern about the time commitment for Andrew. Andrew shook his head and said he felt he had the capacity, plus he planned to delegate as much as possible to me. Again, more laughter."

Ben interrupted, "So you got the top two business continuity program roles identified. Did anyone have any objections to being on the steering committee? Did anyone identify any gaps?"

"I specifically asked whether the people in the room were the right participants for our new steering committee. I explained the role, time commitment, and the long- term nature of the committee. Shannon started by saying that she and Andrew met outside of the meeting and thought this was the right group. She asked whether we should have someone in communications and procurement, but the group felt the committee was the right size, and both communications and procurement report to someone already on the committee.

"Jokingly, or perhaps in a passive-aggressive comment, Melissa Zak told the group that, originally, she wasn't sure she was needed but was afraid that, if she didn't participate, all of her areas of the business would be descoped from the program. The grouped laughed and assured her she was needed. I could tell by Jacob's body language that he wasn't sure he wanted to participate, but he didn't verbally object. I think Andrew and I would have been prepared to argue for the need to have him represent the legal side of issues. Regardless, the conversation ended, and we concluded we had our steering committee."

Ben asked, "So did you get around to asking for their support to engage representatives throughout the business?"

"Yes, I explained that I wanted the steering committee's help in nominating process or department leaders that I could engage with to complete the next steps in the planning process. I explained my time estimate for these representatives and what I needed. The only pushback I got was that I might be underestimating the time commitment, but they told me they would endorse my plan even if the time commitment doubled."

"That's fantastic, Michael," Ben concluded.

"One more thing, Ben. Not sure we talked about this much, but beyond the consensus on the four questions, I think there was a fifth unexpected outcome. Initially, I didn't think that the steering committee was on the same page on what business continuity really means, in terms of what it should deliver to Felder and its customers, and also what it doesn't typically address.

"Ultimately, the steering committee agreed that, for Felder, the purpose of business continuity will be to proactively work to decrease the likelihood of operational disruptions but also work to minimize downtime when a disruption occurs because of a building issue, a people issue, an equipment issue, an information technology issue, or a supply chain issue. They also agreed that the outcome of the effort needs to include a strategic crisis management and crisis communications process, team, and plan that could help organize the response to a disruptive event but could also be used for other types of crises, such as product recalls or reputational issues."

I told Ben that I suspected that the members of the steering committee weren't initially on the same page on this, but it now felt that, if interviewed individually, they all would define it almost identically. I could see how the dynamics of this meeting were essential to getting everyone in alignment. One-on-one meetings could never have accomplished it.

"I concluded the meeting by talking about some of the next steps I had planned— which you gave me, obviously, and I don't fully understand just yet—including the engagement plan, process documentation, and the BIA. The group had no issues at all with these steps. I also promised them an updated copy of the steering committee charter I started."

Ben took a deep breath and started in, "Well, it wasn't easy to get the meeting, and although Melissa pushed back, it sounds like you got what you needed, Michael. Are you ready to begin preparing for the hard part?"

There was an awkward pause, partly because my heart sank as I thought I had already tackled something incredibly difficult. But before I could comment, Ben laughed. "I'm just playing with you. Honestly, getting an executive team engaged and on the same page is arguably the most difficult part of the process. But now we need to engage one level deeper. Should we set up a time to meet and discuss this?"

We set aside an hour on the next day.

Chapter 12

The Engagement Plan

The Journey – Status and Time Check

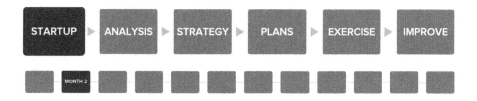

Ben and I met in a small, third-floor conference room the next day at 9 a.m.

I was still flying high over how well the Frame Meeting had gone. Getting the entire executive team on the same page and willing to devote appropriate time and resources to the project seemed a vital key to success. Ben told me that the next step was to formulate what he called an engagement plan, and to be honest, I was a bit confused. I had just finished a highly 'engaged' meeting and secured commitment for a long-term project. Wasn't that a plan?

As I was taking a sip of my coffee and getting ready to express my confusion, Ben started right in, "Michael, we set up this meeting mainly because I want to help you understand the bridge between what you learned from the executive team in the Frame Meeting and how you need to engage the rest of the business to implement the Business Continuity Operating System.

"When I developed and implemented the BCOS at Creden ten years ago, I created something I called the engagement plan. It's a simple tool to identify the different groups involved in the business continuity program and decide how often I, as the program manager, should meet with them, what messaging I should deliver to each, and what I needed to get from each of the stakeholders via these meetings. You probably heard me talk about this in one of the webinars. I'm confident you'll find that making an engagement plan for Felder will make a huge difference in helping you succeed.

"The goal of the plan is to develop some muscle memory and the appropriate cadence to keep all the parties engaged, energized, and motivated to be active participants as we build and continually improve business continuity for Felder. That's the engagement plan. It's that simple."

Listening to Ben describe the engagement plan, I couldn't help but think of my initial challenges in launching the ERM program at Felder. Shannon had told me then that my presentations were theoretical and didn't resonate with the audience because I hadn't related the ERM benefits back to Felder and its leaders. And Ben was now offering a solution to ensure I didn't make the same mistake with business continuity. Plus, if I failed to be intentional about naming the different interested parties and describing how often to engage with them, it would probably feel like I was constantly in a reactionary mode and herding cats. I could see that documenting and publishing an engagement plan would help me feel in control and help the others understand how they fit into the program. Of course, simple concepts don't always equate with easy, and creating the engagement plan reflected this reality.

Ben said, "When addressing any initiative, including business continuity, I've learned that it's valuable to step back and clearly define the different stakeholder groups, what they care about, and how often I should engage them. If I don't do this with business continuity, their focus slips away, I may fail to address their needs, and they might drift away from the work necessary to get the organization prepared for a disruption. Ultimately, they forget that business continuity is a priority for the company. The adage 'out of sight, out of mind' applies here.

"By the way, the engagement plan is also a proactive way to deal with the resistance to change that is a natural part of the BCOS process. The people you want to engage already have jobs and areas of responsibility, so they are naturally at risk of getting overwhelmed and may push back."

Ben continued, "I think it would helpful if I shared a couple of thoughts on the best meeting types for an established business continuity program. You may, of course, need to adjust these meetings during Year One. Are you ready for the overview?"

Again, I nodded.

Ben continued, "Once the program is established, you'll want to have four types of regular meetings. I call them the Focus Meeting, the Monthly Stakeholder Meeting, the Quarterly Management Review Meeting, and the Annual Meeting. Let's review them one at a time.

"The Focus Meeting is for the program manager and any full-time core team members assigned to you. I know there's no full-time core team at Felder right now, but please bear with me for the overview. The Focus Meeting is typically a biweekly meeting designed to build relationships within the team, align on scorecard performance, and resolve issues using brainstorming and decision-making techniques. I'll explain in a few minutes how this meeting can still benefit you and add a lot of value.

"The Monthly Stakeholder Meeting is for those involved in planning and response. In other words, this meeting is for anyone who owns a plan or group of plans. You'll want to meet with these stakeholders every month to build relationships within the extended team, align on scorecard performance, and share best practices, including how to use plans and drive continual improvement.

"The Quarterly Management Review Meeting is for the steering committee, including appropriate representatives from operations, finance, IT, human resources, internal audit, and risk management. You'll want to gather these leaders together on a quarterly basis to align around past program performance, set goals for the quarter, and solve more of the strategic issues impacting the business continuity program's success.

"The Annual Meeting is for the steering committee and often other members of the senior leadership team. This yearly check-in has a similar purpose and agenda as the Quarterly Management Review Meeting, except that the group will be reviewing performance over the past twelve months and planning for the year ahead rather than the next quarter.

"In summary, that's the structure of the engagement plan that worked in Creden's established BCOS. We identified the right people to participate in each meeting and explored their unique needs to be addressed. It's important to know that we also identified other stakeholders that need to be engaged outside of these four meetings. Customers, regulators, and employees in general fell into this 'other' category.

"What we need to do in our time together this morning, Michael, is figure out whether this is the right structure and the right cadence for Felder. We also must identify the people you really need to engage in this effort and in these meetings. I'm confident I don't have to remind you that you are an army of one right now!"

"Yeah," I said, "I'd appreciate that. I have noticed that I'm an army of one." I leaned back in my chair and looked at the ceiling while reviewing what had been decided so far. "We've confirmed that Andrew is the program sponsor with overall accountability. I'm the program manager with responsibility for the day-to-day operation of the program. And we have a steering committee who will act as advisors to Andrew and me, keeping us and the program on track.

"I learned a lot from the Frame Meeting, and I see the value of regular input from our steering committee. But I'm a little confused about the Focus Meeting because I'm not a full-time business continuity resource, and I don't have any direct reports focused on business continuity. I'll only be talking to myself in those biweekly meetings, if I understand this meeting correctly."

I paused and thought about it for a minute and came up with an idea.

"Maybe I should set up a thirty-minute biweekly check-in with Andrew to talk about what's working and what's not. We could review our short-term goals and actions and determine whether we're on track. Essentially, this meeting approach would enable us to address any issues sooner rather than later."

Ben responded, "I do think you should continue to use me as an ad hoc mentor, coach, and advisor, and I welcome you to do that. But given that you are the only one truly focused on the business continuity program, I think you should implement the Focus Meeting approach for you and Andrew.

"For the foreseeable future, you probably won't have a team focused on business continuity here at Felder because we're not big enough for that. If you did have a team, these Focus Meetings would be for you and your direct reports to make sure that you're sustaining momentum continuously."

I asked, "Are you also suggesting that I implement the Monthly Stakeholder Meeting approach? And if so, is it intended for business process owners?"

Ben answered, "Yes, that's exactly right. Imagine getting the process owners together and saying, 'Joe in manufacturing has had some great success doing X, Y, and Z. Joe, do you mind telling Beth, Lindsay, Carl, and Tom about your success? They might learn a lot from you on this, and you might have something we can extend to other business areas. And Lindsay, you talked about a challenge you've been having. Let's process that as an issue and see whether the others can provide some input to you on how to resolve the issue.'

"The Monthly Stakeholder Meeting is about what's working and what's not, and you want to create a forum where participants are talking and sharing and it's not just you talking. This meeting will also include some training content delivered by you. For example, you'll continue to clarify expectations and process issues. Again, it's all about continual improvement.

"One more thing. These meetings also create the opportunity for you to ensure that the entire business is following your process over the long term. That's what 'process followed by all' means under the Startup process. Carefully hold everyone accountable to following your process, not just during Year One but over the long term as well. And if they're not following it as documented, process the problem as an issue during these monthly meetings."

I responded, "That sounds great. I see what you mean about creating a cadence through Monthly Stakeholder Meetings. But can I rename it? Not sure I love the name."

Ben was quick to respond, "Yes, call it whatever you think works best. I'm not prescribing names for these meetings. Call them whatever works; just make sure you stay consistent."

With that question answered, I continued, "Alright, this thing you're calling the Quarterly Management Review Meeting . . . am I oversimplifying by saying it's a quarterly check-in with the steering committee to review program performance, prioritize continual improvements, and review scope and objectives?"

"No, you're not," Ben answered, "that's all it is." After a pause, he said, "Michael, as a reminder, do you remember when I asked you to look at ISO 22301?"

When I nodded, Ben went on, "Remember, ISO 22301 calls this form of engagement a management review. I think it's a powerful tool, and that's why I leverage the same process, with some minor expansion. That means I like to engage the steering committee in discussions that I call 'issue processing.' If we have a strategic issue holding us back from getting to the right level of resilience, I engage them to get their input on solving for the root cause. Having their participation helps with input, but it also helps them take ownership of the issue—and I find they participate in the solution long after the meeting."

Ben waited as I wrote myself a note to do exactly that. I said, "That makes perfect sense for the Quarterly Management Review Meeting, but I'm confused about the Annual Meeting. Don't I have most of the executives gathered each quarter?"

Ben said, "You do, Michael. You have most of the executives on your steering committee, and you're engaging with them quarterly. Still, there are a couple people whom you need to update annually and assure them you're meeting their expectations."

Puzzled, I asked, "Like whom?"

Ben responded, "Well, our CEO, Corey, for example. He's not on the steering committee. Might it be appropriate to touch base directly with Corey once a year, rather than just go through Andrew? Also, think about the risk committee of the board of directors. They might be interested in the investment Felder is making in business continuity. It's a good idea to make sure they're comfortable that we're managing operational risk appropriately."

"Ah, I see," I answered. "This clarification is really helpful, Ben. I appreciate the clear structure. These regular meetings ensure momentum continues, the right people stay informed and committed, and issues are resolved quickly and efficiently. But what about Paulsen and our other customers? Should I schedule meetings with them? After all, Paulsen is the main driver for our program, at least for now."

"Don't worry about keeping Paulsen and other customers informed," answered Ben. "That's not your job. There are already channels in place to communicate with customers, and you might want to engage with our customer relationship managers to discuss this form of engagement."

"Okay," he continued, "now you know the purpose of the engagement plan, with specified meeting types and frequency. Of course, this isn't meant to be written in stone. The timing may change between Startup and Improve. For example, we may end up saying the Management Review Meeting needs to occur monthly because of the volume of work and we want to speed up the program implementation. Does that make sense?"

"Absolutely," I responded. "Formulating the engagement plan will help me avoid a lot of mistakes that could easily occur in a long-term project involving diverse and busy groups of people. I guess I should draft an engagement plan and run it by you and Andrew before I formalize it and share it with the steering committee for their endorsement. And then I can share the plan during our first Monthly Stakeholder Meeting. I need that group's endorsement too, especially since I will need to engage many of their people."

"That's right," said Ben. "As you can see, you'll be facilitating a lot of meetings for the foreseeable future! I'm not sure how you feel about that role. When I worked at Creden, I developed a guide for great meetings. I don't want to insult you by suggesting you don't know how to run a meeting, but I'm happy to offer the guide as a resource."

I smiled and said, "Ben, I'll take any help I can get." I made a note to look for this guide from Ben and began to close my notebook, grateful that Ben had once again given me what I needed, and then some, to move forward with this project.

As I gathered my things, Ben said, "Wait, Michael, there's one more thing we need to talk about right now."

I gave Ben my full attention. "Okay, let's hear it," I said.

"It's time to set some goals," Ben said. "We need to establish strategic goals for Felder's program—for the next quarter, the next year, and the next three years. I'm not suggesting that you need to identify those goals right now. You'll probably want to talk to Andrew about goals during one of your initial Focus Meetings. You'll want to set and communicate goals so that the different groups can help complete those goals. After all, that's what real engagement is about."

Chapter 13

Process Documentation

The Journey – Status and Time Check

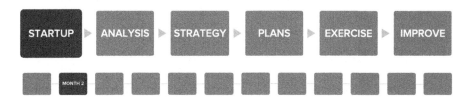

Realizing that it was almost time to embark upon the second phase of the BCOS, Analysis, I set up a short meeting with Ben to review one last topic under Startup, namely process documentation.

Ben and I had briefly discussed process documentation over the past few weeks. He mentioned that most business continuity standards note the need for a policy statement as one form of mandatory program documentation. Other mandatory or recommended forms of process documentation describe how to perform the business continuity process (with the intent that such documentation would set and then enable program participants to consistently meet expectations). I recalled that Paulsen asked whether we had a policy statement and whether they could review it. Ben had also sent me some example files, one of which was a policy statement.

Prior to my meeting with Ben, I reviewed the example policy. It seemed straightforward. The key topics covered were program objectives (what the organization intended to achieve with the business continuity plan) and a scope statement (which products/services were in scope and out of scope, and why). The bulk of the policy statement described program roles and responsibilities, which summarize the content of my engagement plan. Lastly, the policy statement explained the key steps in the business continuity process and the desired outcomes the business should work to achieve. I thought his example, only two and a half pages, did a good job of setting expectations. I could also see why Paulsen would want to see a copy of it, because it neatly summarized the design of our business continuity program.

I also reviewed the business continuity SOPs. This document was lengthy, at approximately thirty-five pages. It appeared to be a how-to guide for the organization to implement the business continuity plan. I was flipping through it when Ben came to my office.

"So, you're ready to move from Startup to Analysis?" he asked with a smile.

I nodded, and he continued, "Well, you're almost ready. We have a bit more to do in Startup to ensure that Analysis goes smoothly. As you know, Analysis is really the first time you meet with the business, outside of the leadership team. Analysis is what many standards refer to as the BIA and risk assessment, which is also when you're going to meet with people representing our in-scope business processes, departments, and activities, and those that effectively own the many resources we need to meet our customers' expectations."

He continued, "As you meet with all these people, they'll want to understand the big picture and what's expected of them during this first year and beyond. This is the reason the BCOS model includes Process as one of the seven key ingredients. You need to have a good idea of what the program will look like, and how it will behave, before engaging with the business. If you don't, it will be difficult to answer expectations-related questions and to get them to follow the process consistently. That said, before you truly begin the Analysis phase, you need to have a defined business continuity plan that's documented and ready to be shared with all program participants."

"That makes sense, Ben. Prior to our meeting today, I reviewed the two sample documents you sent to me a few weeks ago, the business continuity plan and the business continuity SOP."

"I'm glad you reviewed those documents. What did you think?" he asked.

"The policy document is pretty straightforward. To me, it seems to be a summary of expectations and a high-level summary of the program design. Did I get it right?"

Ben nodded and then asked for my thoughts on the SOP.

"Well, it felt like a series of instructions. I took it as a how-to guide on implementing the policy statement. But it wasn't clear who the audience is."

Ben sighed. "This was one of my biggest early mistakes with the BCOS. I intentionally gave you a long, unnecessarily detailed SOP, and it was one of the worst documents I created. In addition to providing too much detail, I literally tried to create a how-to guide for every role, all in one document. And even worse, I tried to make every person in my company a business continuity expert, even those who didn't need to be."

This time I was smiling. "Okay, I'm a little relieved because I thought you did everything perfectly the first time!"

Ben rolled his eyes. "Far from it."

I continued, "Are you saying your biggest lesson learned was to keep it simple and create process documentation to help people effectively participate in the program—but no more than that?"

Ben nodded. "And it needed to be packaged in a way that didn't intimidate the reader. I also wanted it to be the first place a program participant would go for help and guidance, rather than calling me. You're right; my biggest lesson learned was to create usable documentation without unnecessary complexity. I also needed to make sure people knew where to find it."

"Okay, that makes sense, Ben. I remember listening to one of your webinars where you mentioned something about 'process followed by all.' So that's what you meant!" I added.

"It's really simple. I mandated that everyone follow the documented process—no exceptions. We didn't have the time to reinvent the process unnecessarily in every part of the organization. I worked to succinctly capture my expertise in that documentation, and I needed to rely on everyone to work the process so we had consistent outcomes that I could measure."

We ended the meeting with Ben suggesting I draft the policy and SOP. He offered to send me a better SOP example and to review my Felder SOP when I had it documented. Then, after it was drafted, he suggested we should get feedback on clarity and simplicity from three people in the business with little business continuity knowledge. And finally, Ben suggested I approach Andrew for his feedback and approval.

Chapter 14

The Bridge between Startup and Analysis

"Alright, Ben. I've done what we agreed to. I've wrapped up the Startup phase, and I think I'm ready to start Analysis. I documented the Year-One program scope that the steering committee decided on during the Frame Meeting, including products, services, and businesses processes. I've now identified which business processes or departments we need to engage to perform business continuity."

Ben nodded.

"Based on your webinars, I've decided to use the interview-based approach for BIA data gathering rather than a survey-based approach. I must admit, I wanted to go a different direction and simply use surveys. To me, surveys feel more efficient and would save me time by avoiding meetings. But I did some additional reading and learned that organizations that take a survey-based approach often have to follow up with interviews because the information gathered is incomplete or poor quality."

Ben responded, "I'm really glad you're taking this approach. You're going to discover quickly that it's much more valuable to engage the business via an interview than a survey. The results are better, and it's also a great way to start engaging different people on the importance of business continuity. And trust me, it's ultimately more efficient too."

I smiled skeptically and continued, "So I've gone ahead and scheduled the sixty- to ninety-minute meetings with each business process or department owner to kick off the Analysis phase. I think I've scheduled the interviews with the right people. I worked with the different steering committee members to identify participants who can speak to strategic department considerations and provide a high-level understanding of activities and the impacts of downtime.

"When I was working with the steering committee members to identify the right interviewees, I asked that the work be done by people who are familiar with the underlying resources, including people, workplace, equipment, technology, and suppliers. In the discussions with some of the steering committee members, we identified people who were too senior and probably wouldn't understand the resource requirements. And in some cases, we also initially identified people who were too junior and wouldn't understand the cross-organization impacts of downtime."

Ben smiled. "Yeah, I've always struggled with that. In some cases, you take a best guess on the right person or invite a few interviewees to attend."

I continued, "Yes, that's exactly what I did. Another mistake I made was forgetting to include the BIA, the meeting agenda you gave me in the invitation, and a plain-English description of the purpose of the meeting. Needless to say, I had a few people decline, and a few others asked what the meeting was about and how they could prepare. Lesson learned. I updated the meeting invitation and even asked for the steering committee members to support this effort within their business areas."

I asked, "So am I headed in the right direction?"

Ben responded, "Absolutely. I bet you're wondering now what you should be talking to them about during those sixty- or ninety-minute BIA meetings, and even wondering what we should be getting out of the BIA."

I smiled. "Exactly. I viewed two webinars that you gave a few years back, which seemed to make sense. I've also looked at the process documentation that we created, meaning the policy and SOP that I created based on the Creden examples. But I still have a few questions about the BIA and the risk assessment."

Ben nodded and invited me to proceed.

"Let me try to describe how I see it. I think we're trying to develop an understanding of each business process or each department's business continuity requirements, as you called it during one of your webinars. The BIA works to determine how long we can be down, what capacity or performance level meets minimum expectations, and helps us identify the right resources needed to be able to contribute to product and service delivery. And obviously, because we're trying to convince someone to invest in business continuity, we need to justify the investment by working to understand the potential impacts associated with downtime. My question is this: how do I get that information from people throughout the business through these sixty-minute interviews so I can summarize it and put the puzzle pieces together?"

Ben answered, "Okay, let me describe the approach for the interview. Because I have a background in several different business disciplines, I happened to choose a tool called SIPOC from Six Sigma. I found that if I'm able to organize my interview around suppliers, inputs, processes, outputs, and customers and then flip it around to start it with the C—customer—I'm able to have a really meaningful discussion with the process or department owner. SIPOC allows me to structure the interview smoothly and collect the information that I need to identify the business continuity requirements.

"Now that doesn't mean I just walk into the interview and ask them to tell me about their customers. That's not it at all. I have a list of probing questions that I ask. For example, I have what I call initial, or level-one, questions, and then I have level-two questions to get to the appropriate level of detail. Not only do my questions get the answers I'm looking for, but the process also gets people talking about things that I might not know regarding threats or risks to their aspect of the business. There's no way I would ever learn these things through a questionnaire.

"So that's how I approach BIA data collection. And if I've scoped the interview correctly, they typically take sixty to ninety minutes. In summary, I take SIPOC, flip it around, and use these questions to guide my discussion. I don't follow it religiously; I see where the conversation takes me. But SIPOC is a guide to provide structure and keep me honest in terms of asking the right questions and getting the person talking."

I nodded. "That makes sense. I've used Six Sigma in previous organizations too, and I'm familiar with SIPOC. I just never realized SIPOC would be a great way to really understand the business and, as you said, collect business continuity requirements."

"I didn't either," Ben continued, "I actually stumbled across SIPOC when I was in a Green Belt project at a previous employer, while I was a new business continuity program manager. During the training, it just hit me that this is a great thing I could add to my own personal toolbox to structure a BIA interview."

Confused, I asked one more question, "Well, I understand this would help me structure a BIA interview. But what about the risk assessment?"

Ben nodded and continued, "Well, this is where we should talk about Year One versus Year Two. In Year One, I like to focus on the BIA discussion in which I cover the SIPOC topics. During the discussion, I sprinkle in two high-level risk assessment–related questions. First, I ask the interviewees where they are vulnerable to disruption. In other words, do they have single points of failure within their workplace, people, equipment, technology, and/or third-party dependencies? If they do, I take it one step further and ask additional questions, such as, 'If that single point of failure were unavailable, how difficult would it be to transition to another resource?' Or I might ask whether they could do the work differently until that single point of failure becomes available once again. That's how I approach a Year-One risk assessment."

Ben explained that doing a granular risk assessment, especially as described in ISO 31000, in Year One, with a large program scope, increases the risk of analysis paralysis, and significant business continuity risks often 'appear' during a strong BIA discussion.

Ben continued, "We can go deeper in Year Two and beyond. We can use a more in-depth, detailed approach that evaluates the likelihood of disruption and the severity associated with disruption, based on the loss of resources and the effect on different business activities. At a high level, when you do this more detailed approach, you set a scale for likelihood and severity, and you leverage the BIA results to rate the severity associated with disruption. For likelihood, we set the scale based on the history of disruption and factors, such as environmental issues and controls currently in place, that help to avoid resource disruption. But remember, in BCOS, we're worried about the likelihood of a disruption that could exceed the recovery time or downtime tolerance."

Ben paused to let me take a few notes.

"My recommendation to you, Michael, would be to perform a risk assessment initially at a high level. Do it as part of the BIA, but also schedule a few additional interviews with your major resource owners. For example, talk about vulnerabilities and controls with the person or team that manages Felder's major facilities. Talk to human resources about their controls in place to address people's single points of failure and cross-training. Talk to our procurement team about how they avoid using single- or sole-source suppliers whenever possible. Find out how they talk to their suppliers about business continuity and whether they have contractual requirements to manage the risk. Talk to IT and work to understand what they're doing to eliminate single points of failure and create appropriate redundancies inside the data center and what they have in place for IT recovery to another location. Talk about their data backup processes and their cybersecurity practices.

"These are the types of interviews and questions you should consider in Year One. And where you see vulnerabilities to disruption, or where vulnerabilities point to the inability to recover in a timely manner, share those with your steering committee. Prioritize those as actions or even goals to improve over time. Does that make sense, Michael?"

Visit
castellanbc.com/felder
for a sample
BIA interview.

I nodded. "That totally makes sense. I think you've outlined a truly pragmatic approach. Again, I can see how you run the risk in Year One of overanalyzing and getting stuck, rather than starting to identify good solutions or strategies to begin to respond and recover."

Ben nodded and made an offer. "Okay, as we've done in the past, leading up to the Frame Meeting, does it make sense for us to do a dry run of what a BIA interview looks like? Would that be helpful?"

I nodded. "Yeah, that would be incredibly helpful. I'd like to do a few practice sessions on my own with your SIPOC questions, and then maybe we could get together to do a practice session focused on the quality department. Would that be alright?"

We scheduled the practice session for two days later.

Chapter 15

Analysis

The Journey – Status and Time Check

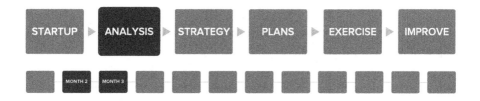

Overall, the BIA and risk assessment process was quite an experience—and a lot of work.

To be honest, it started out a little rocky. I had a few no-shows and had to do some rescheduling. I also had some interviewees show up unprepared, having not reviewed the meeting agenda in advance. Because of that lesson learned, I emailed all remaining interviewees twenty-four hours in advance of our scheduled meeting to remind them to perform the preinterview work and come prepared for the discussion. And not surprisingly, my interview approach was a little choppy at first. I found I focused more on my interview facilitation approach than on what the interviewees were saying. Over time, it got better, and in addition to achieving the outcomes I set for the BIA and risk assessment, I had a great opportunity to learn the business.

I completed the interviews in six weeks and asked Ben to meet with me to discuss next steps.

As I was waiting for Ben, I sat in my office reflecting on something Ben shared in our first meeting, the day after Andrew 'corrected' my thinking on business continuity. I had been fuming about the assignment, not wanting to take the time to 'do' business continuity the right way. Ben had predicted a win-win, however, believing this new assignment would help me quickly learn more about Felder, which was important not only for business continuity but also for the insurance and ERM aspects of my job. All in all, he was right, and secretly I was thankful for the assignment.

I began the conversation by summarizing the steps I'd taken so far. "Okay, Ben," I began. "So, I completed all the interviews. Based on our previous discussions, I've documented the results and produced the reports at a process or department level. I presented the results to the people I interviewed and incorporated their feedback. The process owners made some tweaks, but for the most part, I got approval on all of the results."

Ben interrupted and asked, "How did you handle the topic of downtime tolerance, or what many people call the recovery time objective, or RTO?"

"Well, Ben, I took your advice. Instead of coming out and asking everyone about how long their area can be down, I asked about the impact associated with downtime, meaning the consequences for our organization as it relates to the delivery of products and services. Based on the information the process owner provided, and considering the downtime tolerances for the products and services we established during the Frame Meeting, I suggested the RTO based on the interdependencies with other processes and departments."

Ben smiled. "That's exactly what I would have done. When I asked process and department owners how long they could be down, quite frankly, they often didn't know. They may not always see the big picture. They also might provide an emotional response. And they certainly don't have the strategic insight you gained from the Frame Meeting."

I continued, "Exactly. What's been interesting is that I've had a few questions regarding my RTO recommendations, and once I explained my reasoning, everybody got in sync. For a few of the in-scope departments, I ended up having multiple follow-up meetings to answer questions and address their concerns, particularly around downtime tolerance. But as of right now, I have all the individual BIA reports approved, and I think we're ready for the next steps."

"Great," said Ben. "Can I share some things I did that worked well?"

"Absolutely. That's what I was hoping this meeting would be about."

"Okay," Ben continued, "one of the most important things to recognize is that each of the BIA interviews you led and documented as a process or department-level report is a puzzle piece. Each interview led to the identification of activities and resources that directly contribute to a product or service. These BIA reports, one for each interview, now describe what needs to be done should a disruption occur in a specific area. The process owners also shared concerns they may have regarding single points of failure or challenges with recovery. But now you've got to look at how all this information fits together, understand interdependencies, and make sure the recovery time objectives align. Although we're not going to do a detailed risk assessment this year, we still need to summarize vulnerabilities to disruption."

After a pause, Ben continued, "Alright, let's assume that we've got the go-ahead and make all of the adjustments to all the process and department BIA reports. So what's next?"

I thought for a moment and offered the following to Ben. "Well, I tentatively scheduled a steering committee meeting for late next week, thinking it might be best at that point to share what I've learned and some preliminary conclusions regarding recovery objectives. I also thought I would share business continuity risks that appear to require remediation, including vulnerabilities to disruption and areas where timely recovery may be difficult."

Ben nodded emphatically. "Absolutely. This is the right time to get back with the steering committee to share what you've learned and get their feedback and approval. It's also a good time to communicate those vulnerabilities that you identified and any known recovery gaps. I'm sure there are quite a few. It would be great to get the steering committee's input on how they would prioritize the remediation actions.

"Remember," Ben offered, "I gave you a couple examples of steering committee presentations that you might leverage to guide the structure of the BIA summary. Perhaps before you offer the BIA summary, you could share what you've been up to since the Frame Meeting. And when you get to the BIA results, remember that this meeting is a two-way conversation, so you'll want to engage the members and ask them pointed questions wherever you need feedback and endorsement. Don't be afraid of awkward silence when asking whether they see any issues or if you have their approval to move forward. Highlight anything that was a surprise to you because it might also be a surprise to them, or it might be an issue on which they want to provide commentary."

I agreed and indicated to Ben that I would keep next week's tentatively scheduled meeting. I also asked to meet with him a few days in advance for a dry run of what I intended to present, just to make sure that nothing that I planned to introduce was completely out of bounds.

"Excellent, that works. But let me bring up one more thing," said Ben. "You've got a bunch of individual BIA reports. I strongly recommend that you put together a short BIA and risk assessment summary report and get it to the steering committee as a preread. Give them specific instructions on what you need from them in advance of the meeting, ask how much time it's going to take to review the report, and ask them to come prepared with feedback, questions, or concerns they may have."

I had already begun creating a summary report and agreed that a preread would make that meeting much more effective.

The following week, I presented the BIA and risk assessment results and recommendations to the steering committee. I reminded the committee of the decisions they reached during the Frame Meeting, as well as some of the product-, service-, and process-level downtime tolerances that they agreed to.

Next, I presented which business processes and departments contributed to the in-scope products/services and who I interviewed. I presented a list of business activities organized either by order of recovery or downtime tolerance. The steering committee really got engaged with feedback and questions. They even debated with one another regarding the potential impacts of downtime. Based on their debate and discussion, we agreed on a few changes, and I adjusted the findings after the meeting.

I also presented a list of applications organized by RTO. Again, we had some discussion and made adjustments based on manual workarounds that hadn't been discussed during the BIA interviews.

Next, I discussed some of the business continuity risks that had been identified.

I presented a list of the twenty-nine commercial products to the steering committee and showed that twenty-three were produced in only one location, and they had regulatory approval to produce only in that one location. I pointed out that, based on the input from the subject matter experts throughout the organization, recovering at an alternative location without preplanning and advanced regulatory approval could take anywhere from six to eighteen months. This was our reality, partly because of regulatory approval, and partly because equipment single points of failure were difficult to remediate because of long lead times.

Even though the steering committee was aware that most customers chose to contract for one location only, my report highlighted the impact on our cash flow if we lost a major commercial manufacturing location, such as Carolina, Puerto Rico, or New Brunswick, New Jersey.

We also discussed adverse events reporting and our strong dependency on the Cleveland office, as this is the only place where this work takes place. Those involved in taking calls and other forms of communication were not equipped to work remotely.

Anne Shoemaker, our CIO, discussed the implications of IT disaster recovery planning. Even though IT disaster recovery is out of scope for my effort, mainly because we were told that IT recovery capabilities were sound, I still collected the application dependencies from the business. When I presented that summary, Anne mentioned that some of these dependencies were out of scope of her team's preparedness effort and needed to be revisited. She felt SAP's recoverability was sound, but that a number of data repositories, the phone system, and even systems that fed payroll would need enhancement.

We ended the steering committee meeting by summarizing some of the shorter-term actions that needed to be worked, namely supplier and IT disaster recovery issues, as well as the adverse events reporting single points of failure. We also set a goal of being able to work through strategy selection and documenting the first draft of the business continuity plans within ninety days.

I also was able to present, at a fairly high level, that the next step was to determine some of the strategies to meet the requirements coming from the BIA and the risk assessment. Specifically, we needed to determine strategy to mitigate single points of failure or where recoverability could take a prolonged period of time. We also needed to put together a strong crisis management process and crisis communications plan and identify recovery strategies for areas where capabilities are currently nonexistent.

All in all, the meeting was a success. The steering committee was engaged, and I was really pleased they suggested some changes, as this showed their level of engagement.

However, I had a real concern. The idea of strategy made sense, and I was generally clear on the type of strategies I needed to help the business identify. I didn't know how to help, and I certainly didn't have a list of all the different options. I was concerned that, with my lack of experience, I would steer the business in the wrong direction.

Plus, the BIA and risk assessment took much longer than I had anticipated, and I was way behind on the insurance renewal process. I had already received approval to delay the ERM implementation, but I needed some help in the insurance area. I planned to discuss this with Andrew during our next Focus Meeting.

To prepare, I began writing down my questions, specifically about how to identify and select the best strategies. I knew I needed some coaching from Ben to think through the different strategy options available to us. Thank goodness, that's when Ben walked in.

Chapter 16

Strategy

The Journey – Status and Time Check

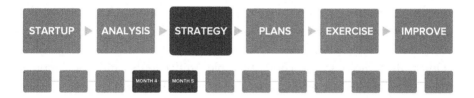

"How did the steering committee meeting go, Michael?" asked Ben. I gave him a brief recap of the discussion topics, the questions that the steering committee members asked, and some of the actions and goals that we agreed to. I even shared with him my concern about how I'd had to ignore my insurance responsibilities, and he agreed this would be an excellent Focus Meeting discussion topic.

Ben then pointed out that he wasn't surprised that the steering committee members failed to remember some of the agreements made on scope, as well as the downtime tolerances agreed to during the Frame Meeting. It turns out this issue is common. Ben then asked, "Okay, so that concluded Analysis. Are you comfortable with some of our next steps regarding strategy determination?"

I went ahead and presented to Ben what I said to the steering committee, specifically, the need for recovery strategies to close gaps that may exist in risk mitigation, response, and communication. I also pointed out that Anne Shoemaker had committed to working on the gaps for IT disaster recovery, and that this effort remained out of my scope.

Then Ben introduced a great source of information that I could use to help determine the strategy. He said, "One of the best ISO standards that's been created so far, or at least the one that has the most practical content, is ISO 22331, which covers strategy determination and selection. There's a great table in that standard that walks through different strategy considerations for facility issues, people issues, equipment issues, technology issues, and even third-party or supplier issues.

"I recommend you review that standard and then see what you can apply to Felder to address some of the issues or gaps that have been identified. Then I recommend reengaging with the same people that you discussed business continuity requirements with during the BIA and explore what might be the best way to recover if the primary resource is lost.

"During those meetings, you could also explore different risk mitigation options to create higher degrees of resilience. What I mean by that is helping to make Felder, or key parts of Felder, less susceptible to disruption. I'm thinking that those types of meetings needn't last too long—perhaps thirty to sixty minutes— and you could also be collecting some of the information necessary to create the first drafts of the business continuity plans for the different processes or departments in scope."

I nodded and told Ben, "This sounds like a good approach. I'll start by reviewing ISO 22331 and scheduling time with the different process and department owners."

Before ending the meeting, I asked one more question, "Ben, when should we start talking about the business continuity plan format? I know it was a few months ago when I made the mistake of thinking that I needed to create a single plan for Felder, and that was all. It sounds like I'll be leading an effort to create a collection of plans, but I'm not exactly sure what those look like."

Ben promised to send me a few plan templates to review, including a crisis management plan, a crisis communications plan, and a business continuity plan.

He also promised to schedule another meeting with me to talk more about the importance of the plan and to explain how plans aren't the most important aspect of the BCOS. To be honest, I was confused but decided to suspend my disbelief until that meeting.

Over the next six weeks, I met with many of the same people that I had worked with to complete the BIA and risk assessment. For each of the process and department strategy conversations, I used a strategy discussion tool Ben provided to guide each of these thirty- to sixty-minute meetings. It was a presentation that helped structure the conversation so the meeting participants could choose the right business continuity strategies for resource disruption.

During those conversations, we revisited the scope of the business continuity program and how the processes and departments mapped to that scope. Next, we explored the five resource dependencies (people, facilities, equipment, information technology/data, and suppliers) and the methods to recover the process or department if those resources were affected. We talked about alternate workspace, alternate staffing, equipment contingency plans, information technology, manual workarounds, and alternate procedures. We also discussed alternate supplier or vendor capabilities, which included different suppliers and even in-sourcing work if applicable.

Outside of the process and department strategy discussions, I worked directly with Ben on the crisis management capability. Ben and I explored the optimal construct of the crisis management team. We discussed how the crisis management team would meet and communicate, and the methods by which they would assess the situation, identify objectives, validate assumptions, and make decisions regarding next steps throughout a disruptive event.

I also worked with Scott Patrick, the head of our marketing team, and BIM and Associates, the firm he outsources much of public relations to, to explore the topic of crisis communications. Using the results from the BIA, we identified different internal and external stakeholder groups that we would need to engage throughout the course of a disruptive event. For each group, we considered the best way to engage them, the information they might want to know, how frequently to engage them, and who was the best internal person to communicate with them throughout the course of the disruption.

Similar to my approach following the completion of the BIA, I scheduled a meeting with the steering committee to debrief them on the gaps between the BIA-derived business continuity requirements and our current-state capabilities. For each gap, I was prepared to discuss the options we considered to close the gap and the recommended strategy and high-level budgetary cost estimates to implement and maintain each.

Most of our discussion centered on risk mitigation opportunities. In particular, we discussed some capital-intensive projects to add resilience at the manufacturing level, which would contribute to decreasing the frequency of downtime. Many of the other strategies did not require resource spend but instead time to document plans and practice through exercises.

Chapter 17

Plans

The Journey – Status and Time Check

Ben came to my office and immediately asked, "I suppose it's time to transition from the Strategy phase and start talking about plan documentation, right?"

I nodded, picked up a pencil, and prepared to take a few notes.

Ben started by saying, "Michael, you remember that I spent five years in the U.S. Air Force, right?"

I nodded, and Ben continued, "What I'm about to share with you about the Plans phase has a little bit to do with my experience in the military, and my experience in general, when it comes to the use of plan documentation.

"It's important to know that there are essentially two schools of thought when it comes to plans, and I happen to sit between them. One school of thought— and this is shared by people brand new to business continuity and perhaps even regulators and people who are methodology 'zealots'—is that plans are the most important outcome of the business continuity process.

"The other school of thought takes the exact opposite view. I think this is where the military mindset comes in. One famous line accredited to General Dwight Eisenhower, which he supposedly said on numerous occasions, was this: 'Plans are useless, but planning is indispensable.' There are many similar quotes out there. For example, one of them goes something like this: 'Plans are only valuable, as they are evidence that planning took place.'

"Like I said, I sit between the two schools of thought. I think plans are important, but I don't think they're the only or most important outcome of the business continuity process."

Ben noticed my confusion. "I can see the look on your face," he said, "and if I remember right, about three or four months ago when you took on this business continuity project, you wrote a plan, took it to Andrew, and thought you were done. As it turned out, there was a lot more work to be done. Am I right?"

I answered, "Yup. That's how things played out, and I'm now enlightened! When I got started, I read a lot of material online that influenced my thinking that the plan was the outcome. But having been educated and coached by you as it relates to the BCOS, I realize there's a heck of a lot more to it. I still cringe when I think of how I embarrassed myself in front of Andrew."

Ben nodded and continued, "Let me share a couple of things when it comes to plans because, again, a plan is just one of the many outcomes of business continuity and the BCOS. First, plans are meant to capture the outcomes of the strategy determination and selection process. For any given process or department, I expect a plan to describe how those responsible intend to respond to a disruption and how they intend to recover from it."

Ben used the whiteboard to list the items that the recovery process and the procedures created to drive the plan should address:

- The initial response and how to employ the strategies addressing the workplace being disrupted

- Both people and equipment being unavailable

- Technology being unavailable or the supplier being unavailable to meet its obligations

As I jotted down the list, Ben said, "That's the number one reason to have plans."

He continued, "There is more than one plan type, and I'll talk about those in a few minutes. The point I want to make now is that all plans should do a couple different things. First, plans should describe what I call the 'commander's intent.' Again, going back to the military, the commander's intent is a concept for military planning in which the commander says something like, 'I want to take that hill,' and that may be the only guidance provided. It's then the responsibility of the military unit to figure out how it's going to take that hill. Think of the commander's intent as the overall objective. In many ways, the commander's intent is sourced from the Frame Meeting and the BIA."

I smiled because this analogy really clicked with me.

Ben continued, "But obviously, the commander's intent isn't the only thing documented in a plan. Let me share three additional things that plans need to address. First, the plan needs to describe how the process or department intends to meet the intent by describing the strategies and outlining how the team should implement the strategies. The best plans include procedures that help implement the strategies or describe how the organization may operate until returning to normal.

"Second, plans need to identify who is going to perform the procedures, including teams and roles to respond and recover.

"And third, plans need to include information that's either difficult to remember or impossible to memorize. For example, it's very difficult to memorize all the team members' contact information or technical instructions to bring a piece of equipment or technology online. Again, very-difficult-to-memorize content represents an opportunity for inclusion in a business continuity plan. I'm going to stop there. Michael, does this make sense to you?"

I nodded, but I still wanted to know more. "That makes sense in terms of what should be in a plan, but I am still wondering how many different plans or plan types I should be creating."

Ben smiled. "Well, that depends on the boundaries of your assignment. Thinking back to the Frame Meeting, we heard a couple different things. One, Felder already has plans that it refers to as emergency response plans, meaning plans that focus on the immediate response to a threat and the protection of people and property.

"That is one plan type, but it's probably not a plan type you need to create. I remember Anne Shoemaker's comment, that IT disaster recovery is out of your scope. She has responsibility for plans to recover infrastructure, applications and other IT services. Many organizations refer to these technical plans as IT disaster recovery plans, and for your assignment, I suppose that's out of scope. But when I think about what the steering committee and Andrew asked of you, I think that there are three different types of plans that are very important. Let me introduce them."

Ben walked up to the dry-erase board and wrote the numbers one, two, and three in a vertical list.

PLAN TYPES

1. Crisis Management Plan
Strategic response to the disruption

2. Crisis Communications Plan
Internal and external communication and coordination

3. Business Continuity Plan
Continue or recover activities following the onset of disruption

"The first one is what I'd like to call a crisis management plan. There are different labels for this type of plan, but think of it as a plan carried out at the organization level, business unit level, or other major organizational entity. Ultimately, this plan type describes how an organization responds to the situation, understands what's taken place, evaluates any assumptions being made, establishes response objectives, figures out the actions to meet the objectives, and prepares to lead and manage the recovery effort. This plan drives the higher-level response process and arms the team charged with leading the response and serving as an escalation point to the process- and department-level recovery teams. So that's a crisis management plan."

I had writer's cramp because of the sheer volume of notes I was taking. Ben paused to let me catch up.

"The second plan is the crisis communications plan, a close relative of the crisis management plan. In fact, depending on the complexity of the organization, you might find that the crisis communications plan is combined with the crisis management plan. Whether this plan is standalone or combined, crisis communications is all about making sure that our organization is in close contact with different stakeholder groups that require an update or with stakeholders that we need to coordinate with throughout the course of the disruptive event. The crisis communications plan summarizes who the different stakeholder groups are, how we stay in contact with them, some of the key message points we need to deliver, how we optimally deliver the message, and who should deliver the communication. The best crisis communications plans include holding statements that serve as templates that can be easily updated to speed the delivery of a crisis message."

I interrupted Ben, "Okay, just to clarify, you're saying that crisis management and crisis communications plans can be different documents, or they can be merged together, depending on the complexity of the organization?"

Ben nodded.

"Okay," I asked, "so who owns these plans?"

Ben smiled, pointed at me, and said, "In the role that you're currently serving in, you do. It's your responsibility to define how to respond and how to communicate. The answers to these questions are clearly outside of your domain expertise, and therefore, you will have to bring others into planning discussions. You're going to need to talk to people who have responsibility for different day-to-day processes and possibly different resources. You'll certainly need to talk to communications professionals about messaging and message delivery, but you have the responsibility for documenting these plans and ultimately making sure that they're socialized, made available to the right people, and maintained."

This made total sense, and I added, "I get it, Ben. At a strategic level, Felder's crisis management and crisis communications plans are a strategic asset and should be owned by the program manager, right?"

Ben nodded. "Yes, that's exactly correct."

Because we were quickly running out of time, I asked, "You mentioned a third type of plan. I'm assuming you're going to bring up the topic of business continuity plans, or what some people call business recovery plans, right?"

Ben nodded again. "Yes. Business continuity plans are typically done at the process or department level. They're designed to summarize the instructions necessary to describe how to recover and how to operate until the process or department can return to normal. Business continuity plans have all the same elements as those we're talking about, including a team that performs the recovery effort to get the affected activities and resources operating at a minimal capability and eventually return to normal operations."

I tried to summarize what I was hearing. "Okay. I'm guessing that the construct of many of these plans, regardless of the type, is probably similar, but the content differs. So each type of plan has a team and a set of procedures that the team performs to accomplish its specific mission, whether that's response, communication, or recovery. Am I getting it right, or have I missed something?"

Ben shook his head. "No, that's really it. And if we go back to our military quotes, the plan serves as a container that summarizes the outcomes of the planning process. But it also does one more thing, which is to give you most of that information in one place. The plan can serve as a reminder when something bad does happen. It's there as a reference to guide the successful and complete response and recovery effort."

I interrupted one more time. "If I go back a few months, which is when I produced the plan template, I learned that we're going to have a collection of plans that will help us respond, communicate, recover, and eventually return to normal. Now I can see where I made my mistake, thinking that it's a single plan and the outcome of the business continuity process is a plan. And I learned that it's ineffective to jump straight to documenting a plan without first discovering how the business operates, identifying its essential resources, and then determining the best strategies to recover following a loss of these essential resources."

Ben smiled. "Yes, and the reason most business continuity program managers choose to have multiple plans is that multiple, smaller plans are easier to maintain than one large one. Think about twenty people trying to maintain the content in one document. That would be hard. If you have a plan owner or contributor mapped to one plan, updates and maintenance are much easier. Plus, the plans might have different uses, which is another consideration."

Another question popped into my mind. "So, like the BIA interviews and strategy that I just completed, I assume it makes sense for me to set up interviews to collect the information I need from the plan owners and contributors. Some of these may be the same people I've been interacting with. I need their input on how they would implement the strategies we just selected, and I can then create the activation procedures as part of their plans. I also need their input on key contacts, team members, and a few more topics. And once the initial draft is complete, I need to get this in front of plan owners to review and approve. Is that right?"

Ben nodded again. "Yes, go ahead and set up those meetings. I'm not sure if you'll need thirty minutes, an hour, or four hours per plan, but I have a feeling that you'll get a good sense of how long you'll need to meet based on the complexity of the strategies that you just identified and reviewed with the steering committee over the last month."

Before I let Ben leave, I thought of one more thing. "Ben, in my research, one thing that came up often was the idea of threat-specific plans, such as plans for a fire, tornado, hurricane, etc. Based on our conversation so far, I assume that's not something you advocate?"

Ben smiled. "You assumed correctly. There's no way to predict all the threats that could lead to a disruption. I recommend the creation of plans that cause a loss of resource, regardless of cause. This is a far more efficient approach. With that said, some organizations, like ours, may want to develop some plan content for threats deemed highly likely. A great example is hurricanes. There are so many actions to take before a hurricane makes landfall, and the creation of a checklist can add a lot of value."

I thanked Ben, feeling armed to tackle the plan-creation effort.

Over the next seven weeks, I worked with the same people I had engaged during the Analysis and Strategy phases to document the initial drafts of their plans. I created the plan 'shells,' and we met to gather the information to fill in the holes. Without exception, each plan owner left the planning meeting with actions to complete and the need to seek approval for the plan.

In parallel with my work to create process- and department-level business continuity plans, I took the lead on the Felder crisis management and crisis communications plans. I primarily engaged with members of the steering committee to get these plans drafted. For the most part, the Felder crisis management team included the members of our steering committee, plus a few additional participants.

At the end of the planning process, I started to think about training and awareness as a prerequisite before we dove into exercises.

Chapter 18

Training

The Journey – Status and Time Check

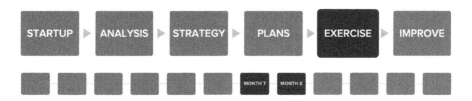

I met with Chris Murphy, who heads up the adverse events management team in Cleveland, to create his department's first draft of the business continuity plan. A few weeks after that discussion, it hit me that we had focused solely on collecting information for his plan. At no point during that meeting did I explain to Chris what his role would be in leading the recovery of his department if the Cleveland office experienced a disruption, if their phone system went down, or if their reporting system experienced some sort of a failure.

I thought back to something that Ben introduced to me during the Startup phase, which was the engagement plan. The engagement plan outlined all of the different stakeholder groups that needed to be engaged and how to meet with them, how to interact with them, what to say, and how often to say it in order to work to solve problems with each group. A key element of the engagement plan is what each program participant needs to know to be an effective business continuity program participant.

I opened the engagement plan and revisited the different groups Ben and I had identified. By and large, I felt the document remained accurate. I thought about the department or process owner, the people named in a business continuity plan, the crisis management team, the steering committee, myself, and even employees at large. I thought about what they needed to know to participate in the BCOS going forward and what they would need to know to effectively respond and recover following the onset of a disruptive incident.

I realized that I had neither the time nor the resources to be able to make all these people business continuity experts in Year One. And for the most part, most of them didn't need to be experts. For example, employees not named in a business continuity plan may only need to know how they're going to receive direction following the onset of a disruption or where to get additional information if they don't hear from someone during a major natural disaster. I could think of other examples.

I thought about the steering committee and how I had gradually helped them understand their role during the Year-One planning effort. But what about their roles moving forward? I thought about the department, or process, owners who had been charged with helping to complete the BIA, risk assessment, strategy determination and selection and, of course, writing the business continuity plan. Did those individuals know what was expected of them as we moved toward the final phase of our Year-One journey, Improve, or during the refresh cycle that would be coming next year, the year after, and so on? Did they understand how they were going to be activated following the onset of a disruption? How were they expected to communicate and coordinate with a crisis management team? Did they understand how to use their plan, how it was organized, and how it could be helpful to them? These were the things that concerned me now.

I had identified more questions than answers, and I needed to think about prioritizing the closure of these questions to make people feel comfortable about the work that had been done over the past six months. And if I ever restarted the ERM program and addressed gaps with the insurance program, I needed to cascade business continuity knowledge out into the business. I shared my concern with Ben during an ad hoc call, and he agreed that it might be valuable to hold some preexercise training sessions with key program participants. Unfortunately, Ben was swamped with his quality work, so it was left to me to come up with a list of training audiences and priorities.

One thing I knew for sure: it was time to figure out how to bring people up to speed. I thought it'd be important to start with revisiting the topic of business continuity. We needed to talk about the outcomes, the value of participating in the program, and where people could go for more information. I also wanted to address the needs of all employees and let them know how they would get more information or direction following the onset of a disruption, particularly if they were out of the office. I thought that would be the logical starting point.

From there, I thought I had better focus on the steering committee. They needed to understand what to expect as we focused on the Improve process so they could cascade that message into their organizations. I figured I'd focus on the crisis management team and, perhaps, deliver some awareness training prior to the first tabletop exercise that I planned for next month. And then I decided I'd better do the exact same thing for the business continuity team leader who'd been serving as the process or department owner in the planning process.

To me, this felt like a good way to prepare for the exercise. But I also recognized that training and awareness-building would be an ongoing effort, and I needed to make a note to refresh the engagement plan and perhaps develop a multiyear roadmap to get all key program participants, and employees at large, to the appropriate competence and confidence levels as we moved forward and implemented the program.

For now, with a focus on preparing for the Exercise phase of BCOS, I identified four training and awareness sessions that needed to take place, each with one specific, strategic objective:

1. **Steering committee**: What will the business continuity plan look like after Year One? For this training, I planned to include it as a special topic in our first Quarterly Management Review Meeting.

2. **Crisis management team**: What are the crisis management team roles and responsibilities at the onset of a disruption? This would be a standalone, thirty-minute training session.

3. **Business continuity team leaders**: What are the expectations of business continuity team leaders, and how do they engage with the crisis management team? This would be a standalone, thirty-minute training session.

4. **Employees in general**: What should they expect during a disruption, and how will the crisis management team communicate updates and expectations throughout the response to the disruption? This would be a short, recorded training.

Chapter 19

Exercising

The Journey – Status and Time Check

I was settling in as Felder's crisis management team coordinator, a role that Ben suggested I occupy in the event that Felder faced a disruption that our business continuity team leaders could not solve and when there was a need to activate the crisis management team.

During the strategy determination and selection process, and while we were writing the crisis management plan, the steering committee and I agreed that Andrew Preston would not only continue to serve as the program sponsor but would also serve as the crisis management team leader. His level of understanding, the respect for him among the different senior leaders, and his decisive decision-making approach would equip him to be successful in managing a disruption that affected the company as a whole. And because of my familiarity with the business continuity program, the strategies that we had selected, the program participants, and all of the obligations we faced as an organization, the steering committee decided I would be the key advisor to Andrew and the rest of the team as we navigated a disruption.

So here we were, about to participate in our first tabletop exercise focused on the crisis management team. As I entered the boardroom, I felt a kind of relief, as the day marked what I considered a major milestone in the BCOS. The business continuity effort was in its eighth month, and we had just completed the first round of training and awareness.

To enable me to be an effective participant and really learn my role, the steering committee decided that we'd have Ben facilitate this first tabletop exercise. So instead of a preparatory session to enable me to plan for and facilitate an exercise, I got to watch Ben live.

Before diving into the exercise, I made the decision, with Ben's endorsement, to spend about thirty to forty-five minutes making sure the entire crisis management team was comfortable regarding the roles and responsibilities of the team, the individual team members, how this team would operate, how the team members would interact with the different business continuity teams, and how the team would also be focused on strategic response, breaking down roadblocks, making decisions when needed, and triggering the crisis communications effort.

Everyone was seated on time at 1:00 p.m., and we began. As promised, I delivered the training and awareness piece, making sure that everyone was generally clear on the team's purpose, roles, and responsibilities. And then I turned it over to Ben, who was waiting patiently in the back of the room, planning to facilitate Felder's first tabletop exercise.

Ben came to the front of the room, introduced himself, and then walked us through the purpose and intent of the exercise. Ben pointed out that this was a safe, sterile environment where we were encouraged to make decisions based on a fictitious scenario that he would be introducing. We would be able to make decisions without the fear of failure. Any failure today would create a valuable learning opportunity that would, we hope, eliminate similar failures during the response to a real disruption.

Ben introduced the rules of the session. Everybody would participate based on his or her assigned role in the crisis management plan. They would consult the plan as a means of validating the content and looking for opportunities for improvement, or even gaps in content. Ben asked that we not judge the accuracy or the realism of the scenario, despite his opinion that it was realistic.

After summarizing the exercise objectives, Ben introduced the scenario. I had little knowledge of what he was planning to introduce. I was curious because this was really my first tabletop exercise, both as an observer and a participant.

Ben introduced the scenario background information via PowerPoint. It appeared that there was a major fire in one of the clean rooms in the New Brunswick, New Jersey, commercial manufacturing location. Based on preliminary information from facilities personnel onsite and the fire department, one of the largest bioreactors in clean room number three had caught fire, resulting in significant smoke, water, and fire damage in the main clean room and in two or three adjacent rooms.

The scenario background concluded with Shannon contacting Andrew to let him know that fire had broken out. Because of the significant impact on the organization and some of Felder's largest customers, she recommended that the crisis management team convene to assess the situation, establish near-term objectives, and think ahead to how we would recover the affected operations in New Brunswick. The scenario also mentioned that everyone successfully evacuated the site prior to the fire department's arrival, and it appeared that no one was injured during the fire.

After Ben introduced the scenario, he looked across the table and said, "Andrew, I'm going to turn it over to you now in terms of the response." Andrew seemed kind of surprised, as if he had expected Ben to lead us through the overall response.

Almost as if he were reading Andrew's mind, Ben continued, "Andrew, I won't be here during a real event. All the work we've done over the last eight months sets you and the rest of the crisis management team up for success to be able to effectively manage a response when activated based on the criteria noted in the plan. So again, let's just practice.

"Let's talk about what the initial response looks like. Maybe I can go ahead and suggest this . . . after Shannon contacts you, you're probably going to be thinking about the need to convene the crisis management team and whether you want all team members involved or just a subset."

Andrew smiled and opened his plan to page five, which was a summary of the crisis management plan, and then looked up to the group. "In this type of a situation, given how important New Brunswick is to Felder and some of our most important clients, I think I'd want to have everyone on this first call. And because it appears that the fire took place at about 6:00 p.m. today, I would go ahead and activate the team and get everyone on a conference call to talk through the overall situation and what our objectives might be for the next few hours."

Ben smiled, nodding approvingly. Andrew continued, "Michael, I'd look to you to use our emergency notification system to contact the crisis management team, while at the same time, just to play it safe, I'd email the crisis management team, asking them to get on the phone in about twenty minutes."

Andrew flipped to page seven in his plan, which was the initial checklist for the crisis management team. I could see he was scanning the procedures to see what was expected of him and the team over the first few hours. I watched him flip to what looked like Appendix II, which was the crisis management team meeting agenda.

Playing my role, I informed the team that I had used the emergency notification tool to send a message out via email and SMS to their mobile devices and had phoned their mobile devices, asking them to get on the conference bridge number in about twenty minutes.

Andrew then took over. "Okay, let's assume we're now on a call together, and let's talk about what this first crisis management team meeting would look like. I would convene, make sure everybody was present, and then ask Shannon, who owns the New Brunswick location, to give us a summary of what she knows, what she's assuming, and ultimately how she sees the event unfolding."

Before Shannon could comment, Jacob interrupted, "I don't mean to be the contrarian, but I need to ask, is this all necessary? Wouldn't the management team in New Brunswick simply work the issue?"

As Ben and I prepared to respond, Andrew took the lead. "I can't remember whether I'm the only one that's been on a crisis management team and participated in a response to a real disruption, but let me share one thing. In responding to something similar to the scenario that Ben just presented, I can tell you that the local site will be chaos, and they will escalate issues and depend on company leadership to navigate much of the customer and supplier communications process. I can tell you, again based on experience, that without a well-rehearsed crisis management process, the response and recovery effort would be delayed, which would result in not only great financial consequences but also much greater reputational impairment as well."

With a still-skeptical nod, Jacob said, "Thank you for the explanation. Let's see how this plays out."

At that point, Ben handed out a damage assessment form that was serving as an exercise inject from the local onsite team, summarizing the facts regarding the fire in clean room number three. As Shannon read much of the information to the team, I could see that Ben was handing out other paper copy injects to other participants in the room. One inject, which was handed to our head of communications, appeared to be some sort of a media inquiry.

Andrew went around the room asking people to offer anything else that they might know, any assumptions they were making that needed to be tested, and any thoughts or input regarding objectives for the next four hours. Once everyone had the opportunity to speak, Andrew summarized what he heard and made the decision to focus on four specific objectives until 10:00 p.m. The first objective was to communicate to all employees that the facility would be closed the following day. The second was to create a press release regarding the fire, emphasizing that our focus was on our people's safety, serving patients from that location, and assessing the situation to understand the severity of the fire. Our third and fourth objectives were to reach out to individual customers to discuss the potential impact on them and to understand inventory levels throughout the pharmaceutical supply system.

With that, Andrew adjourned the team and instructed everyone to get back on the phone at 10:00 p.m., local time, with updates on these four objectives and any other situation updates that Shannon collected from the onsite team.

After about ten seconds of silence, Ben interrupted. "I thought that was very well done. It was well-organized, succinct, and, by the way, highly unusual for a first tabletop exercise and first meeting to be able to consider all of the information coming at you at a very rapid pace." Ben then advanced the PowerPoint presentation to see all the different review questions based on this first scenario to assess what had been covered and what may not have been covered. As it turned out, with the exception of setting up a debriefing with the employees in New Brunswick that might have been affected, the first crisis management team meeting met all of Ben's planned discussion topics, which, by the way, were taken from the crisis management plan.

For the next two hours, we explored multiple elements of the advancing scenario and discussed how the crisis management team supported commercial manufacturing, business development, and many other client-facing services. As in an earlier steering committee meeting, the crisis management team discussed the lack of off-site recovery for a number of products and how surprised Felder's customers would be when they received the news. Some exercise participants were surprised, particularly those not on the steering committee, which led to an objective to create one-on-one crisis communications talking points for the account management team when they reached out to customers.

We also revisited our goal of mitigating impact, the effect on patients, and the impact on the clients for which we're producing products. Last, we talked through how best to restore the New Brunswick facility and see whether anything could be transferred effectively and quickly to any other location.

For the last fifteen minutes Ben led a debriefing, asking every individual what had gone well and what could be improved. He wanted feedback not only on the exercise session but also on the crisis management plan, the crisis management team, the business continuity strategies for New Brunswick, and commercial manufacturing as a whole.

These were the top three lessons learned:

1. Rehearse communication to employees using many different methods, including the new emergency notification platform

2. Create a crisis communications template or holding statements for use by account management to engage affected manufacturing clients

3. Add a crisis management team role for an account management representative

Ben promised an exercise summary report that would also detail some recommended short-term actions and medium- to long-term goals to drive continual improvement.

Before we concluded the session, Andrew requested another exercise using a hurricane scenario, given the upcoming hurricane season and the importance of our operations in the Caribbean. With that, we adjourned.

Based on informal conversations I had as people were leaving the session, steering committee members thought the time was extremely valuable and hoped that we could do something similar again. Even Jacob seemed pleased. Several participants mentioned possibly working through an exercise with a different scenario within three months, so we could continue to advance the maturity of the crisis management process.

After everyone left, Ben and I discussed my observations on how well the exercise had worked. Ben asked me an important question: Would I be comfortable conducting such an exercise at the process or department level to get people comfortable with their roles as business continuity or business recovery team members and to identify opportunities for improvement at the business continuity plan level? I told Ben I had absolutely no choice but to give it a shot, recognizing that I didn't think it would go nearly as smoothly as it would with him as facilitator, at least at first. I hoped that after I had a few exercises under my belt, I would get very, very comfortable.

As it turned out, I was right. The first two or three department-level tabletop exercises weren't great, but I think they were effective. My biggest lesson learned was to talk less and encourage the participants to talk more. The fourth through tenth tabletop exercise sessions were great. Over a span of a few weeks, I gathered close to thirty short- to medium-term continual improvement actions to drive higher levels of preparedness.

Chapter 20

Paulsen's Feedback

Steve called, letting me know that I needed to be available the following week to meet with the Paulsen team to review our business practices, including business continuity. We had received conditional approval to begin contract manufacturing on their behalf, but it was contingent on their getting comfortable with three issues, the first being business continuity.

When Steve called to ask for my participation in the meeting, he reminded me of Paulsen's requirements. He said, "As you know, they have business continuity requirements, and I'm certain we meet them now. They don't want to pay for multisite manufacturing capability right now, but they want to know that we have the capability to recover an affected manufacturing location's capacity in the event of a major catastrophic event. With our goal of placing their manufacturing in Carolina, they are concerned about the threat of hurricanes. They also want business continuity protections for anything that supports manufacturing and protections for us to successfully run Felder. They want us to follow a specific standard, meaning ISO 22301, and they want the right to audit us on a periodic basis."

Steve continued, "We're meeting next week, and I'd like you to present the program to Paulsen's team, highlighting what we've done and what we plan to continue doing." I agreed and planned for the meeting accordingly.

The following week, when I entered the conference room, three serious-looking people, plus Steve and Shannon, were already present. I connected my laptop and provided an overview presentation of the business continuity program now in place at Felder. Perhaps fifteen minutes into my presentation, the people from Paulsen seemed to relax. When I was done, they asked a few questions. One was about the scope of the tabletop exercise and what we had learned from it. Another asked how we were measuring our compliance with our process documentation that described the design of our business continuity program. Finally, they wanted to know our plan to continue maturing the work that had been performed over the past eight to nine months.

I was confident in my answers, and the Paulsen team members were highly engaged throughout the discussion. When they asked for a copy of the plans, I offered to show them right then and there. I opened the online plan repository that I created, showed them a list of the plan documents, and opened the crisis management plan and the commercial manufacturing business continuity plan. Again, they seemed pleased.

One of the Paulsen participants, Julie Baker, asked a very pointed question as we were wrapping up the meeting. "How long do you think it would take to recover our manufacturing capacity elsewhere if the Puerto Rico site experienced a catastrophic hurricane?"

I sort of expected Shannon to ask Steve to take the lead in answering the question, but they looked to me. I took a deep breath and gave it a shot. "As I understand it, your intent is to seek FDA approval to commercially produce the product solely in Puerto Rico. Based on our work during the BIA and Strategy phases of this year's planning effort, we could be up and running in Ireland in about six weeks, which includes some manufacturing expansion efforts. However, the biggest unknowns are the regulatory approvals. This is where we would need to have some advance conversations with the FDA, and we would need to have some immediate coordination with the regulators following the onset of the disruption. That aspect is beyond our control, and therefore, it is difficult to answer your question definitively. But for the work solely under our control, we could be ready to manufacture in six weeks."

I could see them taking notes, and once she finished, Julie looked at me. "The prolonged regulatory approval process is clearly a concern, and while we work through the decision-making on multisite manufacturing, I think it would be of value to have a joint tabletop exercise to work through roles and responsibilities in engaging the FDA."

I nodded, as did Shannon and Steve. Julie smiled and indicated she had no other questions.

As the hour-long meeting was wrapping up, I asked for their feedback and whether anything had made them uncomfortable, other than the manufacturing recovery point that we had set an action to address. All three shook their heads.

With that, I excused myself, thanking them for their time and promising updates whenever they requested them. As I was walking out, I saw Steve and Shannon look at one another, both with smiles on their faces.

Chapter 21

Getting Ready to Improve

The Journey – Status and Time Check

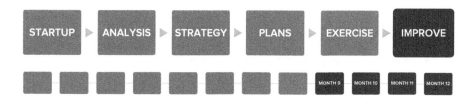

I had completed Analysis through Exercise in about eight months. With Paulsen generally happy with the outcomes, we landed their contract manufacturing work. Although I felt good about the results of the business continuity work performed to date, Ben told me I was far from done. In looking at the list of actions and to-dos that I'd accumulated, I knew he was right. Plus, Paulsen had reminded me three times in our meeting last month that I needed to maintain the business continuity outcomes and fully implement the strategies we had identified. I knew they would periodically check in with me to evaluate progress.

Beyond the actions and to-do items identified, over the past eight months while we worked to design and implement the Year-One business continuity program, the business had already changed. We had acquired two smaller contract manufacturer competitors, neither of which had a business continuity program.

Additionally, Andrew had just announced a significant acquisition that would be closing in six weeks. Felder was purchasing Medina Therapeutics, which maintains the patents for three phase 3 type 2 diabetes therapies, one of which Felder was already producing in a contract manufacturing capacity.

From Ben's recorded webinars, I remembered that part of the BCOS includes a repeating phase that he called Improve. I still had the URL to that recording, so I typed it into the browser, fast forwarded to minute thirty-five or so, and started to listen.

While Ben was talking, he displayed a slide titled Improve Phase with seven bullets:

- Measure

- Goals

- Actions

- Focus Meetings

- Quarterly Management Review Meetings

- Annual Meeting

- Check It

Ben then presented information on each of the seven processes. After I took notes, I decided to email Ben to set up a few meetings to clear up some questions. He replied that he had some time the next day between 3:00 and 4:00 p.m.

Chapter 22

Business Continuity Measured and 'Actioned'

The Journey – Status and Time Check

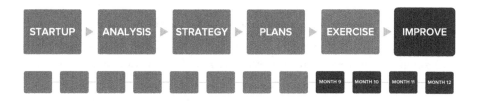

Before he even sat down at my desk the following day, Ben got down to business. "You mentioned you watched an old BCOS webinar and had a few questions about the Improve process."

I had a good idea of where I wanted to start. "Over the last nine months, while we've been working on the program design and implementation, you've used the words 'issue processing' over and over, but I never asked you to explain. Until now!" I smiled.

In his dry tone, Ben started in, "I'm actually a little disappointed it took you until now to ask, especially since you've been having Focus Meetings with Andrew and Monthly Stakeholder Meetings with the different process owners!"

I sarcastically lowered my head in shame.

Then he smiled. "You've had a lot on your plate, and I'm truly glad you raised this now. The concept of issue processing is crucial to high-energy engagement with different program stakeholders. It is core to the idea of continual improvement."

I took out my BCOS journal and started taking notes.

Ben continued, "You're already getting a tremendous amount of business continuity feedback from many different sources: meetings, the business, the steering committee, the risk assessment, exercises, audits, scorecards, Paulsen, and many others. When something fails to meet expectations, I consider it an issue, and we need to find the root cause behind the issue so we can solve it, for once and for all, and work quickly to meet expectations."

Ben paused, probably because he saw me struggling to write everything down.

After I slowed my note taking, he continued, "Remember when we first introduced the seven core BCOS ingredients—Frame, Process, Participation, Engagement, Measurables, Improvement, and Automation? It turns out that those seven ingredients are also the seven root causes of poor business continuity performance. We want to reserve as much time in the Focus, Monthly Stakeholder, Quarterly Management Review, and Annual Meetings to process issues. And when we have the right issue processed in the right meetings, people stay engaged because they are actively part of continual improvement. That's what I mean by issue processing. There are myriad ways to process issues. We can cover that in depth later if you like."

I pushed back, "Can we roleplay processing an issue? I want to make sure I've got it."

Ben agreed and asked me for an example issue to process.

"Here's one. The person responsible for business continuity in our clinical trials area isn't doing a good job and is consistently late with everything. And in some cases, he just doesn't show up to meetings or is not responsive."

Ben smiled and nodded. "Okay, of the seven BCOS ingredients, which most closely aligns with this issue, in your opinion?"

I thought about it for a minute. "Participation is probably the ingredient or, as you called it, the root cause."

Ben asked, "Why?"

I explained that I thought the person assigned to do the work either didn't have the time or didn't want to do the work, and therefore he was probably the wrong person.

Ben nodded. "This is a very small example of issue processing. Perhaps this is an issue processed during a Quarterly Management Review, with the action being to find the right person or helping this person with the 'want it' or 'capacity' constraint."

I nodded and thanked him for going through the example. Ben's explanation made sense, so I moved to the next topic I wanted to cover: Measurables. "The idea of metrics and scorecards makes sense to me. This isn't something applicable only to business continuity. Is that what you meant by 'Measure' in your webinar?"

Ben got out of his seat and walked up to my dry-erase board. "Michael, there are two types of metrics you should consider. I think we may have briefly talked about these when I introduced you to the BCOS. First, there's the product and service. Based on the scope of the program that the steering committee provided input into during the Frame Meeting, you might choose to measure Felder's ability to recover each product or service that our customers have charged us with implementing business continuity for. You could also measure the timing associated with recovery based on what we have in place. When I was at Creden, I measured our anticipated ability to transfer manufacturing from one location to the other by product so we could understand our exposure, and we could then use the information to prepare for customer discussions."

Ben also suggested that I measure precommercial production single points of failure by product. As with commercial products, I should measure the anticipated transfer time to restart production somewhere else if the primary production location were to fail. Because clinical trials management was in the scope of our program, he suggested that we measure how much downtime we were likely to realize in the event of a Cleveland office disruption and the strategies we would put in place to transfer the work to another Felder location. We should do the same thing with adverse events reporting management. Ben felt that we should again be talking about the maximum downtime we could expect based on the strategies in place for alternate workspace, alternate staffing, and information technology recovery.

Ben pointed out that I should go through this process to evaluate each of the in-scope products and services. I should prepare to present a scorecard to the steering committee during Management Review Meetings. He would explain the format later.

Ben concluded his discussion on metrics and scorecards by pointing out that I should consider which metrics to present during each meeting, based on what the attendees would be most interested in, and which metrics would influence change the most.

I know I had a skeptical look on my face when I asked a very leading question. "Not everyone's going to care about product and service metrics. I know lots of people are going to want to understand whether they did all of the business continuity tasks assigned to them. Am I right?"

"You are absolutely right, Michael. The other metrics we need to define are activity- and compliance-related metrics. These metrics help identify whether the business continuity process is performing as designed and the organization is fully engaged and following the process described in the process documentation."

Ben went on to suggest that we measure and report on the completion of activities such as the BIA, the completeness and currency of business continuity plans, and the completion of exercises. He also thought we should report on overdue corrective actions and where we saw poor engagement with different stakeholder groups, as described in the engagement plan.

Ben continued, "Focus Meetings are a great place to review activity and compliance metrics. When things are off, Focus Meetings help us figure out why and take appropriate action."

After we were finished talking about metrics and scorecards, Ben wanted to talk about other inputs to make the meetings described in the engagement plan as effective as possible. "Michael, there are essentially three types of continual improvement efforts: Goals, Actions, and Experiments."

He paused and discussed the topic of goals. "You should also work with different program participants to define goals, which might consist of a few quarterly and annual goals to move the preparedness effort forward."

Ben and I had a good conversation about what an annual goal might be, and we decided I should talk to Andrew about getting the three new acquisitions through the Analysis to Exercise processes within the next twelve months.

Ben also suggested that a ninety-day goal could be to create a repeatable supply chain risk management process that engaged our vendors to understand their business continuity capabilities, especially given the importance of our vendors in our day-to-day operations. He also suggested that each of the department-level program leaders create goals specific to implementing and validating recovery strategies.

"Ben, the term Actions is unclear to me. What does this really mean?"

Ben explained that Actions is a broad term describing commitments coming out of different meetings in response to solving issues, implementing solutions to improve metrics, and addressing audit and customer feedback regarding the program.

"Ben, you mentioned Experiments during the webinar as a means of driving continual improvement and engagement. What does that mean in the context of the BCOS? When I first heard you mention the concept of Experiments back when we first met, I thought it sounded like a fad or something. Is this really the most important thing to focus on now?"

Ben answered, "Think of Experiments as a low-risk way of getting people to try out solutions to solve issues and, even if unsuccessful, learn from the experience. When I was at Creden, we encouraged people to come up with their own experiments and implement them, getting others to volunteer to participate. We found that people would often debrief on their experiments during the Monthly Stakeholder Meetings. I discovered that experiments could deliver great stakeholder engagement. I understand you may not see the importance of it now, but perhaps toward the end of this initial planning cycle, as you approach Improve, you might find it is a tool that can add some value."

I looked at the clock and realized we were out of time. Ben said he would be out the following week at a conference, but he could meet on following Monday to cover BCOS meetings in greater depth.

Chapter 23

The Engagement Plan in Action

The Journey – Status and Time Check

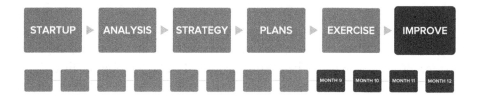

When Ben returned, we got together as planned. The purpose of the meeting was to address some of my additional questions about three of the four BCOS meeting types. Now that I had wrapped up the business continuity program design and the first-year implementation effort, I considered the program in continual improvement mode. Ben really sold me on the engagement plan, especially the monthly, quarterly, and annual meetings.

Throughout my assignment as Felder's business continuity program manager, I had been using Ben's Biweekly Focus Meetings to engage with Andrew to set expectations and process issues. I was still the only person truly focused on business continuity in a near full-time capacity. Andrew remained the program sponsor.

Ben then asked me, "During the webinar, did the meetings component make sense, and specifically, how might you engage the different groups here at Felder?"

Visit
**castellanbc.com/
felder** to listen
to a sample
Focus Meeting.

I paused for a moment, and then based on my recollection of the webinar, I suggested the following: first, I should continue having Focus Meetings every other week with Andrew as the program sponsor to make sure he was aware of what the program was doing, review scorecards and metrics, revisit the priority of all identified actions, and also perform some issue processing.

Ben seemed to agree, so I continued.

Then I thought a little bit about the Monthly Stakeholder Meetings. Given the number of process owners throughout the business that were participating in the program on a part-time basis, I decided it was important that I connect with them. I wanted to understand, on a monthly basis initially, what was working and what was not and create a platform through which they could direct questions, to me or to one another, and share what was working well for the benefit of the others. During those meetings, we might be creating to-dos, setting goals, and ultimately closing some of the existing actions identified during the first eight to nine months.

Again, Ben seemed to endorse my thinking and asked me to remind him I requested some sample focus and monthly meeting agendas that might benefit me. I nodded and continued.

The third meeting type that I had in mind was the Quarterly Management Review Meeting with the steering committee. Ben's webinar content on this was straightforward, and he reminded the audience that ISO 22301 has a management review process with a structured approach to review performance of the program, review corrective actions, seek input on the prioritization of those corrective actions, and address any roadblocks preventing an appropriate level of resilience.

Again, Ben nodded and endorsed the idea that the ISO 22301 management review is a powerful process and appropriate for Felder's steering committee.

I then described to Ben my understanding of the Annual Meeting with the senior leadership team, including Corey. I believed the purpose was to be able to talk about goals for the program, any major scoping changes in general, changes to the answers to the four Frame Questions, and any major strategy changes that Felder was about to encounter that would impact the program. During that meeting, based on information presented to me, I would suggest certain goals that I could then fine-tune and execute under Andrew's direction.

Ben again nodded and then offered a summary, "You are at the point now where you should fully implement the engagement plan and the four meeting types. Constantly evaluate whether you have the right people in the right roles. Measure, process issues, and set actions."

I nodded.

Ben offered one last point, "I think you've accomplished a lot, and quite frankly, it was fun for me to engage again in business continuity."

He stood up, and I thanked him profusely and immediately started to brainstorm how best to demonstrate my thanks. I certainly owed him! Before leaving, I offered to help anytime.

Preparing for the first Monthly Stakeholder Meeting required a lot more than I had anticipated. I created the following meeting agenda based on Ben's example:

- Scorecard (5 minutes)
- Actions (5 minutes)
- Training (20 minutes)
- Issues (25 minutes)
- Conclusion (5 minutes)

We had eleven process owners who were coordinating business continuity efforts for their departments, and I invited them all to the meeting. I met with three of them beforehand to help structure a scorecard that would interest them, which mainly involved activity and compliance metrics to help highlight which activities were, and were not, performed. Some of the process owners thought they would like to hear about product and service metrics, and we agreed to present these once a quarter. For the activity and compliance metrics, we agreed to report and review the percentage of BIAs approved, percentage of plans approved, and percentage of exercises performed.

One of the business process owners, Judy Walker, who has responsibility for process development–related departments, had experienced incredible success in engaging her departments. So I asked whether she would be willing to lead the training discussion and share with the group how she got 100 percent on-time participation in all of the major planning activities.

I also began to create an issues list for the group. I decided to ask the process owners for their input during the meeting, but I was ready to identify at least three issues:

1. How to get BIA and plan owners who really wanted the assignment

2. How to increase efficiency with the review and update of BIA and plan documentation

3. How best to deliver employee awareness training and the right topics to cover over the following three months

After all this preparation, I was ready to facilitate the first Monthly Stakeholder Meeting. Of the eleven process owners, eight attended. Two declined because of work travel or PTO, and one didn't show up.

We reviewed the scorecard, and everything was generally on track, so we didn't add any issues to the issues list.

Judy did a fantastic job, and the other seven attendees peppered her with questions about what she was doing well and how they could apply her approach in their areas.

I thought the issue processing was just so-so. I kicked off that portion of the meeting explaining what Ben had explained to me about seeking the root cause and solving for that. I showed the group the seven ingredients—Frame, Process, Participation, Engagement, Measurables, Improvement, and Automation. At first, they really didn't seem to understand. But when we covered the first issue (how to get BIA and plan owners who really wanted the assignment), three of them said they had multiple people participating who didn't want to lead the planning effort for their departments. We discussed why and strategies to motivate and each agreed to an action to schedule one-on-one meetings with the department representatives to discuss whether their lack of participation was due to 'don't get it,' 'don't want it,' or 'capacity.' We also agreed to review the results during the next Stakeholder Meeting.

The meeting time flew by, and I asked each of the eight participants to rate the meeting on a scale of one to ten. We averaged an 8.2, and the one person who rated the meeting a seven offered feedback that she wished she'd been given an opportunity to provide issues in advance and to prioritize the list. I thought that was good feedback.

Chapter 24

Refresh

The Journey – Status

About three days after my first Stakeholder Meeting, I got to my desk and noticed a voicemail from Ben.

"Hey, Michael, during our meeting yesterday, I forgot to cover one more thing, but I don't think it warrants another meeting unless you see it differently."

He continued, "I meant to cover the topic of refreshing the work you've performed over the last nine months. The refresh process includes reviewing and updating the Frame Meeting, which I recommend performing during your Annual Meeting. It involves reviewing and updating the process documentation based on lessons learned from the previous year.

"You'll also want to refresh the results from Analysis, evaluate the Strategy selections, update Plans, and perform Exercises, including training and awareness sessions."

In the voicemail, Ben also recommended using the Analysis through Exercise methodology to address the program scope expansion resulting from the three newly acquired businesses and the regulatory advisory services area that the steering committee asked to include in scope during Year Two.

With that, Ben ended the call and invited me to set up a meeting if I had any questions about his voicemail.

Chapter 25

Check 'It' and the Annual Meeting

The Journey – Status

I hadn't seen Ben in a while, and it had been about eleven months since we designed the business continuity program, so I was surprised when he knocked on my office door.

"Sorry for dropping in on you, but do you have a minute?" I stood up, shook his hand, and invited him to take a seat.

"There's one more thing I want to cover with you, Michael. Remember when we covered the topic of metrics? I forgot to mention something during that meeting. I created an assessment to help measure the strength and maturity of the business continuity program based on the BCOS attributes. In many ways, the overall rating is a measure that you can track over time to help identify actions to improve focus, engagement, and the outcomes of the planning process."

I asked, "I think I remember you covering this in an article or presentation. Did you call it something like the Check It assessment?"

Ben nodded and pushed a piece of paper over to me. The paper listed twenty-five questions, and beside each question were the numbers one through four.

"The assessment is simple," he explained. "If your BCOS is very strong in relation to that specific question, give yourself a four. If it's very weak or nonexistent, give yourself a one. And then add up the numbers for all twenty-five questions. You'll get a rating of twenty-five to a hundred."

I looked over the questions and was tempted to answer them for Felder right then, but I decided to wait.

"Michael, look at the back of the page. I've given you a key to assess trends based on your answers to certain questions. For example, if you scored low for questions twelve and thirteen, you might want to really dig into how you are measuring."

He invited me to answer the questions and then debrief with him. He also suggested I review the results with Andrew to give him a sense of the progress in the past eleven months.

Before leaving my office, Ben asked whether I scheduled the Annual Meeting with the steering committee and Corey. I admitted that I hadn't yet, and I added that to the issues list I had created for my next Focus Meeting with Andrew.

Ben reminded me about the default meeting agenda for the Annual Meeting and reminded me to think about who should attend. He suggested that I first consider engaging the steering committee and then add other members of the executive team. In our case, he strongly recommended we invite our CEO, Corey, to the meeting, especially since he had been a strong proponent of business continuity when we first got started.

Ben walked up to the dry-erase board and jotted down the recommended Annual Meeting agenda in green marker.

- Check-in (5 minutes)

- Program summary (10 minutes)

- Product and service dashboard (10 minutes)

- Key risks, high-impact actions, and issues (20 minutes)

- New annual + quarterly goals (10 minutes)

- Conclude (5 minutes)

I reviewed this agenda and the topics with Andrew at our next Focus Meeting. Andrew endorsed the idea of bringing the steering committee together and also agreed that we should add Corey to the meeting. He asked that I prepare the materials and send the presentation to him one week in advance, and he promised to review and provide feedback. He also promised to schedule the Annual Meeting the week after next.

The meeting was here before I knew it. I sent materials to Andrew, who had a few comments and questions for me to address.

The meeting was at 9:00 a.m. in the Felder boardroom. Corey arrived about two minutes late, but the rest of the steering committee was on time. When Corey was finished settling in, I began.

I reminded everyone that this was our Annual Meeting of the business continuity program and introduced the agenda. I began with the check-in and asked that all participants spend a moment answering a simple, two-part question specific to the business continuity program: What's working and what's not working? The attendees took a moment and scribbled a few notes, then I went around the room.

As people spoke, I added their responses to the table I had prepared on the whiteboard. I offered my input too, as I had grown accustomed to engaging the group and trusted that I could be candid with my feedback.

Name	What's Working	What's Not
Shannon Carter (COO)	Transparency regarding Felder's level of preparedness	Concern about the customers' understanding that they need to pay for manufacturing recoverability
Anne Shoemaker (CIO)	Her team's happiness with the receipt of IT disaster recovery requirements	Concern about the investment necessary to meet the business's expectations
Steve Henry (SVP, BD)	Paulsen's pleasure with the progress	Same as Shannon
Jacob Cunningham (SVP, GC)	Feeling better about meeting customer contractual requirements	Rumblings about the time commitment from the businesses participating
Jack Tanner (VP, HR)	The employee crisis communications process	Employee training and awareness
Melissa Zak (VP, SS)	Her team's commitment to creating actionable recovery strategies	Should we be concerned about getting certified?
Andrew Preston (CFO)	This team's commitment and willingness to tackle roadblocks	Same as Shannon and Steve
Corey Smith (CEO)	The progress made in eleven months; Paulsen's reaction	Surprise regarding the manufacturing recovery responsibility issue
Michael Taylor (VP, RM)	Management support and engagement	My capacity to do my other work

I suggested, and the group agreed, that we add the topic of manufacturing business continuity to the issues list for discussion. Andrew requested we add my capacity concern to the list too, which I did.

Next, I presented the business continuity plan summary. I had four slides, one for each of the original four Frame Questions. I asked the group to review each question and their original responses. There was no feedback on the drivers, but we had a great discussion on scope. We agreed that the scope for Felder remained accurate, but I asked the group whether the work performed by our new acquisition, Medina Therapeutics, needed to be added.

Corey was the first to speak up. "Absolutely. Not only is this a strategic acquisition, but the product we produce now has a major impact on the lives of those with diabetes. If our drivers remain the same, we would be hypocritical not to address this key business."

There was a lot of nodding, so I moved on.

We reviewed the 'how much tolerance' question, and again there were no changes. However, I asked the group the same question I had asked eleven months earlier: How much downtime would you tolerate for the three products produced by Medina? We reached consensus on four weeks because of an off-site safety stock of finished product.

Last, we discussed the program roles. Except for the issue of my personal capacity, and Jacob's concern about significant levels of business participation, we agreed that no other changes were necessary. Shannon confirmed she could represent Medina Therapeutics because she had spent a considerable amount of time with them over the past months.

Next, we reviewed the product and service dashboard I created to compare the downtime tolerances from the Frame Meeting to what we could currently achieve after Year One. I kept it simple, mainly because I wanted to get their feedback on the approach. Ben had been clear that I needed to put something together that would create discussion and then solicit feedback from the group.

Product/Service	Downtime Tolerance	Current-State Capability
Commercial manufacturing	2 weeks	(Red – Does Not Meet Expectations) Customer and product specific
Precommercial manufacturing	1 month	(Red – Does Not Meet Expectations) Customer and product specific
Clinical trials management	3 days	(Green – Meets Expectations) 1–2 days
Adverse events reporting management	4 hours	(Yellow – Partially Meets Expectations) 8 hours
Process development	2 weeks	(Yellow – Partially Meets Expectations) 2–4 weeks

Not surprisingly, this topic created a lot of conversation, mainly around how I could estimate a current-state capability when we hadn't done too much testing yet. I explained that I had formed an opinion in collaboration with the process owners, assuming a worst-case scenario that involved no notice of the disruption.

Corey was again drawn to the red-light status for manufacturing, and I reminded the group we planned to discuss this during issue processing, which was our next item on the agenda.

For the next twenty minutes, we covered the two issues identified so far: manufacturing continuity and my time constraints to address business continuity, ERM, and the insurance program. As Ben had suggested, I presented each issue, suggested a root cause based on the seven BCOS key ingredients, and facilitated a discussion in which the meeting participants asked questions. Once the questions were over and we reconfirmed the issue, we identified the actions required to close the issue.

For the manufacturing issue, we agreed that customers may not realize that they need to consciously ask for off-site recoverability. We would need to remind them that, should Felder experience a catastrophic failure, it could take six to eighteen months to recover their precommercial or commercial manufacturing without a second-site capability. Shannon and Steve jointly took the action to work on presale communications content and discussion material for our existing clients. Shannon also took the action to explore how to create a cost-effective multisite production capability to lessen the financial burden on our clients. She was correct in pointing out that we could use this strategy for Medina Therapeutics's business continuity capabilities once we added them to our business continuity program.

For my capacity issue, I presented my professional challenge in getting all three of my responsibilities done in a high-quality manner. I explained that when I first received the business continuity assignment, I didn't want the responsibility, but that my attitude had changed since I truly appreciated the importance of the work and could see how it tied into our business strategy. After a lot of discussion and brainstorming, we agreed that instead of splitting up my role, we would look to hire a full-time business continuity manager who reported to me. I wasn't sure how I felt about that, but I agreed, nonetheless.

Shannon added one more issue to the list since we had about three minutes left in the issue processing portion of the meeting. She brought up Carolina, Puerto Rico, and her concern about the hurricane threat and how important the work performed there had become—and added that Paulsen's manufacturing was now at that location. She suggested we spend some time talking about how to manage the risk and avoid "putting all our eggs in one basket" (as she put it). Andrew began to object by pointing out the financial benefits of implementing business continuity capabilities, but we were out of time and agreed to table the discussion for a future meeting.

The last ten minutes of the meeting were reserved for strategic goal setting. I suggested two goals I anticipated would be supported for the next year:

1. Build presale communications to influence business continuity implementations (Steve and Shannon)

2. Add Medina Therapeutics to the scope of the program within the next eight months (Me)

Based on the issue processing, we identified two more:

3. Hire a business continuity program manager within four months (Me)

4. Create a multisite manufacturing strategy for board consideration (Shannon)

We agreed to monitor the progress on goals during our Quarterly Management Reviews with the steering committee.

Since we were out of time, I moved to conclude the meeting. I reminded everyone that we each needed to rate the meeting from one to ten, and if the score was eight or below, we would offer a way to improve it. I asked Corey to go last in rating the meeting. After everyone else rated the meeting, which was a mix of nines and tens (with one eight from Steve because he felt we should have spent more time on customer messaging). Corey gave the meeting a nine. He smiled and said the content had been both enlightening and engaging. But it was his last comment that I thought was most important.

"I really want to thank all of you for tackling the issue of business continuity. It's true that Paulsen woke us up to the need, so to speak. But I think we all realized this was important. I'm glad Paulsen is pleased with our work, but as we just discussed, we're far from done. It's clear to me that you all recognize this effort is not a one-and-done thing, so I ask you to continue to engage on this important topic. Andrew, please keep me in the loop, especially with any roadblocks that I can help in removing. I think the goals we just set are strong and necessary. I will update the board next week during our quarterly meeting." With that, he stood up and left.

Chapter 26

The Response to Hurricane Cooper

It was near the completion of Year One of our business continuity plan that we learned, four days in advance, that most of the hurricane prediction models were forecasting that a growing storm would likely threaten Puerto Rico. Over the years, there had been glancing blows from hurricanes, but none caused significant damage for us. Since 1980, ten named hurricanes had hit Puerto Rico. With this threat, we were in completely new territory. We had known this day might come, but the financial advantages that led to the selection of Carolina, Puerto Rico, as Felder's largest commercial manufacturing location outweighed the risks by a long shot.

And there we were, preparing to convene our company's crisis management team within thirty minutes in response to the threat of Hurricane Cooper. This would be our first formal meeting in response to the hurricane, although over the past seventy-two hours, I'd spent nearly 100 percent of my time on calls with customers and our COO's team.

Because of my role at Felder, I received the hurricane alerts and began sharing high-level information with the senior leadership team as well as the leadership team in Puerto Rico. Because of the decision to concentrate a significant percentage of our manufacturing capacity in Puerto Rico, many hurricane preparedness action plans were already in place for such a threat, and strategies were in place to acquire additional materials sourced from Puerto Rico for our

U.S. and European locations. We also had procedures in place to move some of our customers' most critical products to other locations in the event of a longer-term failure—if they had contracted for such a service. The focus of our plans, however, was on taking care of our people and protecting equipment and raw materials from wind and water.

The forecasts proved true, and within a day, we were facing the arrival of Hurricane Cooper, a category four, slow-moving hurricane with maximum sustained winds of 142 mph. The eye was forecast to cross the northeast coast of Puerto Rico, very near our manufacturing location, early the following morning. Robert Taverez, Felder's general manager responsible for operations in Puerto Rico, had closed the plant and directed employees to follow government orders regarding evacuation. According to an email from human resources, over 40 percent of manufacturing staff were in an evacuation zone, and the government predicted significant rain and power outages beginning today.

Andrew Preston, our CFO and the crisis management team leader, entered the conference room—about twenty minutes before our crisis management team meeting. As Andrew moved to his chair at the head of the table, he looked at me and said it all in two sentences: "Well, a lot's gone into this business continuity effort. Let's see how you did."

I think I sank into my chair a bit. *How I did . . . ?*

By design, I had spent more time with Robert Taverez than with any other business continuity plan owner. Because of the hurricane threat, combined with the importance of the Puerto Rico location to our company, I worked with his leadership team to really think through how to make the site as resilient as possible. When we first got started, I was surprised to learn that this location didn't even have backup power for the bio reactors, and no plans were in place to protect equipment from flood waters (where practical). A lot had taken place since then, and we were very well prepared—or as prepared as we could be—for a hurricane. We hadn't yet tested our backup power generation—we scrambled to get it in place, as the implementation effort was supposed to extend into next month—and our account management team had not yet held the customer awareness sessions with all customers regarding the need to consider off-site manufacturing capability for their most critical, time-sensitive products.

"Okay, let's get started, everyone." Andrew convened the crisis management team meeting, which he would officially chair for the first time, after practicing with two exercises last month. Andrew is comfortable in this role, and his performance organizing the meetings was amazing. In my opinion, he has many of the skills that effective crisis leaders have. He brings focus to the team, is concise and incredibly organized, and he excels at setting objectives and managing by them. Despite the potential consequences associated with this storm, having Andrew at the helm appeared to make people feel somewhat at ease.

We were convened in our emergency operations center, which is on the second floor of our corporate headquarters. CNN was playing on the TV in the corner, although on mute. The screen showed rain and surf pounding the northeast coast of Puerto Rico. In addition to Andrew and me, also present were Shannon Carter (COO), Jacob Cunningham (general counsel), and Jack Tanner (human resources). Several others—Anne Shoemaker (CIO), Steve Henry (business development), Scott Patrick (marketing/crisis communications), and Melissa Zak (strategic services)—would be joining via conference call.

Andrew continued, "As a reminder, we will be following the agenda on page sixteen of the crisis management plan. Michael, would you provide a brief situation update to get the group on the same page as to what we're facing?"

"At a high level, our operations in Puerto Rico are being threatened by Hurricane Cooper, a category four hurricane with maximum sustained winds of 142 mph. The eye is forecast to cross the northeast coast of Puerto Rico, very near our manufacturing location, early tomorrow morning. Our plant general manager, Robert, closed the facility thirty-six hours ago and directed employees to follow government orders regarding evacuation. Over 40 percent of manufacturing staff are in an evacuation zone, and the government is predicting significant rain and power outages beginning today. Due to expected telecommunications issues, Robert is unable to be in this meeting, and he's evacuating further inland with his family."

I continued, "Because our general manager can't be on this call, I'll summarize what we've done so far. If you'd like to follow along, the hurricane preparation playbook is Appendix I of our crisis management plan. I've also detailed the completion of these tasks online in SharePoint as a situation report, which you all have access to. Please search for a file titled Hurricane Cooper Situation Report."

I reviewed the list of actions that Robert and I had ensured were completed over the past four days:

1. Fully refuel the generator, which we installed and tested last month

2. Test satellite phones provided to the general manager and head of human resources in Puerto Rico

3. Cancel all recurring inbound and outbound transportation

4. Close the hurricane shutters

5. Request updated contact information for all employees and provide them with an overview of how to obtain updates from management, assuming power and telecommunications are available

6. Confirm everyone understands how to evacuate, and ensure that everyone at risk has a safe place to go

7. Cover, using plastic tarps, all critical equipment susceptible to water damage

8. Remove all equipment and materials located outside that could 'take flight' in a wind event

9. Move as much as possible from the ground on the first floor

10. Ship all finished product to the inland warehouse or to New Brunswick, New Jersey, via air

11. Move all raw materials to the inland warehouse

12. Shut down IT systems

13. Put the site on lockdown prior to evacuating the security staff

14. Confirm availability of advance team to perform the damage assessment when given the 'all clear' by the government

15. Assess Cork and New Brunswick readiness for expanded production of the three client products with contingent regulatory approval for production at those locations

I paused and asked whether anyone thought we had missed anything.

Melissa Zak, via conference call, was the first to speak. "Have we engaged any of our local vendors in Puerto Rico regarding their preparations? If I recall from the BIA and risk assessment we performed, we have a critical vendor about twenty minutes from the plant that supplies product that we keep in short supply."

She was right; we did have a critical supplier on the island and in proximity.

"Melissa, unless I'm mistaken, I think we overlooked this," I said. "It's certainly too late to engage procurement to purchase an extra supply of the bio reactor filters from MisTech and ship them to New Brunswick. We'll do our best to engage them following landfall, and we'll mark this as a lesson learned. As I recall from the BIA and risk assessment, this is the only local supplier we're concerned about."

Andrew moved us along, "Scott, do you want to give an update on our crisis communications efforts?"

Scott nodded. "About three days ago, I worked with Shannon to draft some talking points for our customers with product being manufactured in Puerto Rico. We have provided those talking points to anyone with a customer-facing role. We also proactively emailed our customer contacts and asked account managers to call them as well. I also worked with Jack on our internal messaging, and I think our people down there are well informed. The main message to our employees was 'Stay safe, home is more important than work, and check in with us as soon as it's safely possible after the storm passes.' We set up an emergency phone number and plan to staff an employee check-in station on or near the Felder property in Puerto Rico. Part of the check-in process is to update us on their families and homes. We're prepared to assist as much as possible."

Andrew interrupted, "I'm so glad we had the hurricane exercise last month. Our lessons learned around employee communications were invaluable."

Everyone in the room was nodding.

Andrew asked a question, "Have we had any employees ask for financial assistance to enable evacuation? I believe we offered that about forty-eight hours ago."

Jack answered, "Yes, we did field eight requests for financial assistance. We also secured hotels further inland for five families and assisted with transportation for six others."

Andrew nodded, and I could tell he was happy we created that process following the hurricane exercise.

Shannon Carter spoke next. "As Michael said, I think we're as prepared as we can be, and we've done an admirable job executing our business continuity plan for Puerto Rico. But there's one more thing that I think we need to update the group on. We have three trucks of supplies staged near the Cleveland airport to depart as soon as the airport opens, and we have trucks on standby in Puerto Rico to receive the supplies. We have construction materials, food, and water, primarily. We also have a second shipment ready in New Brunswick in case we need to ship replacement raw materials, parts, and supplies. We also have numerous volunteers who have offered to go down to help with cleanup—homes included—and to staff operations if we're able to resume before our employees are."

I looked around the room and saw everyone nodding.

Andrew took control of the meeting. "Okay, unless anyone has something else to offer, I'd like to continue."

Silence.

"Okay, we've covered the status update portion of the agenda. Now let's transition to assumptions and objectives. Based on my assessment, we're now assuming we will be hit with a cat four, and we probably won't know much for about twelve to eighteen hours, possibly not even until sunrise the next day. We're expecting significant damage caused by water and wind. However, based on flood plain analysis and structural engineering analysis, it won't be a catastrophic loss. We're also assuming the inland warehouse is fine, and the airport will open inside of thirty-six hours after landfall. We're assuming our employees are aware of the risk and have evacuated inland, but our biggest issue is absenteeism due to anticipated damage to homes and personal property. Have I missed anything?"

Jacob spoke up. "Just one small thing. I believe we have cameras in the plant, and our security team here will monitor them continuously. However, we're assuming we'll lose power and network communications, right?"

Anne Shoemaker agreed.

I added that we all hoped we would continue to have the camera feed for situational awareness purposes, but the assumption was accurate.

Andrew asked one more time whether anyone else had input. Everyone in the room shook their heads, so he continued, "Okay, I think our objectives are pretty straightforward. We're on standby until the damage assessment team reaches the site. At that point, we will assess the situation based on the team's feedback and prepare the air shipment. Everyone agree?"

Again, nodding.

"Okay then. Let's conclude the meeting with some action items. First, Michael, you are responsible for the online situation report, and once we have actionable information, you will convene the crisis management team. Shannon, your security team will monitor cameras and take any calls from the damage assessment team and local management, and then engage Michael and me when you learn something. And your team is also preparing for the air shipments. Unless there's anything else, let's adjourn."

Chapter 27

Learnings

About a week later, five and a half days after Hurricane Cooper's landfall, the local population was still suffering the effects of a historic, catastrophic storm. The hurricane's eye reached land as a category four storm, but luckily moved inland and back out to sea at a fairly rapid sixteen miles an hour.

Our crisis management team met twice daily for the first three days, and then once a day over the next two days. Andrew decided we would continue to meet at noon each day to ensure our support levels remained consistent.

Fortunately, our plant experienced only minor damage. We had lost power and telecommunications, as expected, and power was still out. We continued to receive diesel fuel from three local providers. A small portion of the roof in the northeast part of the building had failed, which resulted in some water damage to equipment. We expected that equipment damage would cause a delay in resuming production for two of our customers, but we've assessed finished product stock levels, and we anticipate we'll be fine there.

The most significant impact was on our people. Twenty-two of our employees lost their homes, and many more had yet to return to their homes due to damage. Because of the minimal damage to the plant, we redirected construction supplies to help our employees. Our human resources team actively worked on contingent housing, and they even served meals out of our cafeteria to those affected, including employees. Nearly forty volunteers flew down to the local area to help, complete with tents and camping supplies.

It took time to complete the post-incident review, mainly because the response was ongoing, but I planned to schedule that session as soon as our crisis management team stood down. But I did look back at the hurricane exercise summary report and the lessons learned from it. As discussed during our initial meeting, we had learned a lot from that exercise and, thankfully, applied those learnings to this response effort.

The top five learnings in the exercise report were:

1. People first, business (a distant) second

2. Decision-making is different; the leadership team will (necessarily) be less collaborative—Andrew is in charge

3. Sustain the business, don't grow it—redirect business development time and resources to the response

4. Proactively communicate to customers and employees, and ensure there is a way to receive updates from employees in the local area

5. The plan became (sort of) important as a set of reminders since we don't face hurricanes that often—build, maintain, and consult checklists

Chapter 28

Value Delivered (Again)

With Hurricane Cooper in the rearview mirror and things generally returning to normal—combined with a bit of a lull in the business continuity lifecycle—I settled into the office on a Monday morning and decided that I should focus on risk management and some of our insurance program renewals. I don't think I was at my desk for more than fifteen minutes when Andrew Preston and Steve Henry, our head of business development, walked into my office.

Andrew began, "Do you mind if we sit down for just a second, Michael?" I certainly wasn't going to say no, so I nodded, pointing to the two chairs in front of my desk.

Steve began, "Michael, we've obviously talked about how a number of our clients, especially those that had been asking about business continuity, are extremely pleased with what our company's done under your direction. The feedback's been amazing. Not only have we been able to answer all client inquiries successfully, but we're now proactively marketing our business continuity capability as a differentiator in the biotech contract manufacturing industry. Quite frankly, we couldn't have done that without you, and I wanted to come by your office just to personally thank you again. As Andrew and I have been talking, we think we have an opportunity to create a case study that we can add to our marketing and business development materials regarding the overall response to Hurricane Cooper. We would certainly like to have your help in doing so."

I smiled self-consciously and nodded. "I'd absolutely be happy to help. That's a great idea."

Andrew went one step further, "Michael, I think our company's overall response to Hurricane Cooper would've been absolutely terrible had it not been for the work that you performed for us over the last year. Not only did we develop an understanding of our blind spots in Puerto Rico, but we also had solid strategies and playbooks to help guide us through and navigate probably one of the most significant disasters ever to affect the island and our organization. We're going to talk a lot more about that later, but I just wanted to pass on my sincere thanks, as well as that from Corey. Your efforts have certainly not gone unnoticed." With that, he stood up, shook my hand, and left the office.

Chapter 29

Back to the Cafeteria

The next day, I met Shannon in the cafeteria for a mentoring discussion over lunch.

The last year had been a whirlwind, and we hadn't met in a mentoring capacity all year. I had set up this meeting to discuss my concerns about getting the ERM program off the ground.

We both sat down, shared some small talk, and as is customary, Shannon made one of her bottom-line statements.

"Remember last year when I shared my opinion that I didn't think you knew the business, and that lack of knowledge might be getting in the way of a successful ERM launch?"

I sighed, and before I could answer, she continued, "That was obviously a rhetorical question. Now, based on your work with business continuity, you understand what we deliver of value to our customers and patients, how we do it, and who's responsible for the core business activities we perform. That knowledge is invaluable, and it helped guide us—and continues to guide us—toward the right level of resilience."

I nodded.

"I'm not suggesting you completely shift your focus to ERM, but I know the senior leadership team is eager to leverage your knowledge of the business, and your knowledge of ERM, to help us prioritize how we manage our entire portfolio of risk, of which business continuity is only one part."

I smiled, and she asked, "What do you need from me to get this headed in the right direction? I'll give you a heads-up: Andrew's planning to ask the same question tomorrow."

THE
BUSINESS
CONTINUITY
OPERATING
SYSTEM
MODEL

Note: As mentioned in the preface, part two of this book is an introduction to the entire BCOS model. The BCOS includes what many would consider traditional business continuity planning lifecycle activities, such as the BIA, plan creation, and exercises. This book is not meant to introduce all business continuity management lifecycle activity best practices or make the reader an expert in the BIA, risk assessment, strategy selection, plan creation, or exercises. Rather, it's meant to address the truly unique elements of the BCOS, or how the BCOS advocates novel approaches to business continuity management.

For those interested in methodology-related best practices or training, we recommend ISO 22301 and the Good Practice Guidelines (GPG) of the Business Continuity Institute (BCI).

Chapter 30

An Introduction to the BCOS Model

The Castellan team has helped build and run hundreds of high-performing business continuity programs—similar in many ways to the story at Felder.

Around 2016, we realized that there are only seven core components to every business continuity program, as illustrated in the model on the following page. In other words, making sure your program has each component is the 'price of admission' to achieve the appropriate level of resilience.

As we performed business continuity program assessments around the world, we discovered that every problem could be sourced back to one of these seven components: Frame, Process, Participation, Engagement, Measurables, Improvement, and Automation.

We became focused on creating processes and tools designed to strengthen these core components to ensure a long-lasting program that delivers great capabilities—and a program manager that finds fulfillment in his or her role. Chapters 31–37 explore each of these components in detail and include our best tools and ideas to strengthen them, all coming together to build a high-performing business continuity program. Chapter 38 focuses on helping you pull it all together. The final chapter is about finding fulfillment in your role as program manager. We want you to enjoy your job!

Note: If you already have a business continuity program, you can use the following chapters as a reference manual. Just keep in mind: *Every struggle, problem, or frustration is caused by weakness in one of the following seven core components.*

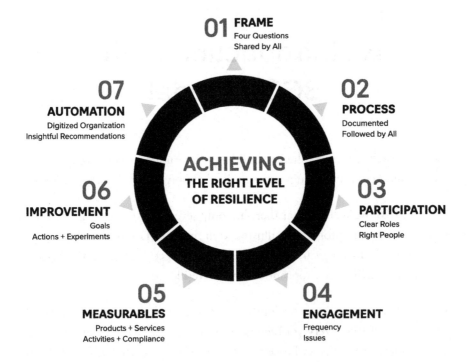

Chapter 31

Frame:
Come to Consensus on the Four Questions

One of the most common problems we see with business continuity programs is lack of focus. You know you lack focus if you answer yes to the following questions:

- Do you feel like you have too many plans?

- Is everything deemed critical?

- Are you lost in constantly trying to justify RTOs?

- Are you unsure who should take part in the business continuity planning effort or if you're allowed to engage the business?

The answer to the problem of poor focus is for you, the business continuity professional (who may be the program manager, the person responsible for business continuity, or a key contributor), to have an effective Frame Meeting with senior leadership to get everyone on the same page with the answers to the following four questions:

- Why are we doing business continuity?

- What are we trying to protect?

- How much business continuity do we need?

- Who should be involved in the program?

This Frame Meeting can happen at any time—but we've found it works best to hold it as early as possible when implementing your business continuity program.

By the conclusion of the Frame Meeting, the program manager will have all the necessary information to drive program focus and truly align the business continuity program to the organization's strategy. The rest of this chapter discusses how to prepare for and facilitate the Frame Meeting and use the information to engage the organization over the long term.

Prepare for a Frame Meeting

Choose participants. Include senior leadership for all in-scope products and services, finance, human resources, and IT. Ideally, Frame Meeting participants have the authority to direct program efforts and the organizational knowledge to answer the four questions.

Finding a time for all participants to meet for a ninety-minute meeting can be difficult. However, everyone needs to be present for the Frame Meeting. The dialogue among participants is key so they can debate and question one another and get in sync on answers to the four questions. Having everyone in the room will save you considerable time down the road.

Conduct a dry run. Many executives expect presenters to show up with answers, not questions. If you go to the Frame Meeting with a blank sheet of paper, will your executives embrace that? To jump-start the conversation, we recommend drafting your own answers to the four questions in collaboration with one or two other key stakeholders (perhaps your program sponsor).

During this dry run, facilitate the meeting just as you would in real time and practice capturing everyone's feedback. This practice approach not only provides a great starting point for the Frame Meeting but it also gives you the confidence to engage your executive leadership team. As you practice, be prepared for some difficult questions from participants.

Conduct the Frame Meeting

A Frame Meeting is most successful when all participants are actively engaged and transparent about their thoughts and opinions. Throughout the meeting, brainstorming rules must apply, and all issues need to be openly discussed. Remember, the point isn't for you to gather the answers to these questions. It's to get everyone on the same page regarding each answer. If the Frame Meeting participants don't agree, you need to give people the space to debate and get in sync.

Let's walk through each of the four Frame Meeting questions, including tips and ideas for facilitating.

Understand the Four Focus Questions

Why are we doing business continuity? The goal with this question is to have everyone sold on the importance of business continuity. It's best if you can connect business continuity to the core mission of the organization. If business continuity isn't perceived as that important, get that on the table at this point to discuss it!

The result of the Frame Meeting should be a list of reasons why business continuity is important, with everyone nodding. This list should include any regulatory requirements or external requirements, such as customer service–level agreements.

Because the term 'business continuity' can mean different things to different people, this question also helps establish an agreed-upon definition and what the program will deliver.

What are we trying to protect? The purpose here is to be clear on the products and services the organization wants to protect. The list of products/services should be:

- Written as actions whenever possible, unless a list of the organization's products and services is well defined and socialized

- Important to external stakeholders

- Precisely worded

- Approximately eight to twelve products and services (for most organizations)

See the following examples.

Good Product/Service	Bad Product/Service
• Manufacture product X • Allow customers to place orders on the website • Process wire transfers • Address customer service inquiries via the call center and email • Dispatch police following a 911 call • Pay employees accurately and on time • Perform insurance claim intake	• Investor relations (not an action and thus too broad; this could be a whole department rather than all the specific people and resources needed to deliver SEC filings) • Ordering (too broad) • Work performed at location Y (too broad; not all work at a location is equal in terms of importance) • SAP (an application/resource, not a product or service)

How can complex organizations have just eight to twelve products and services to protect? Focus on what's most time-sensitive and think in terms of products, services, or core business processes that add value to key stakeholders. Here is an example for a hospital:

- Protect and help patients in residence

- Provide trauma services

- Provide centralized services (lab, pharmacy, imaging)

- Staff the call center to triage and schedule

- Send out health records

- Provide outpatient services

- Pay employees

- Bill patients and collect

Don't worry about getting these perfect. They will change over time and get fine-tuned, and some may be removed.

How much business continuity do we need? The purpose of this question is to assign downtime tolerances to the products and services identified as needing protection. The answer to this question doesn't have to be precise; it just needs to get everyone on the same page regarding how much downtime, if any, the executive team can tolerate. Keep in mind, the answers need to be independent of any existing business continuity capabilities, formal or informal, the organization may already have in place.

The easiest way to answer the question is to ask the room to shout out a timeframe from a list and see whether disagreements come up. Once everyone is on the same page, it's time to move on. Don't try to get it perfect; you'll revisit these conclusions during the BIA.

The benefit of collecting this information is that it gives you a preliminary list of executive expectations. There is no need for an exhaustive quantitative cost analysis to justify a downtime tolerance. The executive team will tell you the preliminary requirements and probably offer high-level qualitative (customer expectations) and quantitative (financial risk) justification.

Who should be involved in the program? The answer to this question helps identify the right people for four key program roles:

- **Program sponsor:** Person engaging executive leadership and accountable for business continuity program performance (this individual is typically a member of the executive leadership team).

- **Program manager:** Person responsible for managing the program on a day-to-day basis. This individual reports directly to the program sponsor and functions as the liaison between the business and steering committee.

- **Steering committee participants:** People who represent the interests of the organization, specifically in-scope products, services, and supporting processes. A person serving on the steering committee provides strategic oversight and support for the program, reviews performance metrics, and helps with prioritizing action items. Limit the size of the steering committee, optimally, to fewer than ten people.

- **Process or department leads:** People tasked with taking part in the planning process and driving continual improvement.

To review whether you have the right people, use the 'Right People' tool discussed in Chapter 33.

Prior to concluding the Frame Meeting, the person leading the meeting should summarize the answers to each of the four questions to seek endorsement from the participants.

Typically, the Frame Meeting should take ninety minutes. However, if the executive leadership team has failed to get in sync on the four questions, you'll need additional time or a follow-up meeting. For your business continuity program to be a success, it is essential that the leadership team gets in sync.

Follow Up After the Frame Meeting

Capture the answers to the focus questions in either a program summary document or a business continuity policy. A program summary can be a document that addresses the program purpose, drivers, in-scope products and services, key program roles and responsibilities, and the departments and functions that align to the in-scope products and services (and the point of contact for each). Instead of a document, you may choose to post such information on an intranet or SharePoint site.

When it comes to the Frame Meeting outcomes, be sure to revisit the answers annually (as part of the Annual Meeting, described in Chapter 34), to ensure the leadership team continues to be in sync with them.

Finally, the products and services identified in the Frame Meeting will serve as a key filtering mechanism for the entire business continuity program. Consider these impacts:

- The BIA can now focus solely on the areas that support the organization's most important products and services. In addition, the BIA can focus more on understanding resource dependencies than on trying to precisely quantify possible impacts of downtime since the bigger-picture downtime tolerances are already set.

- Response and recovery strategies can focus on the dependencies of in-scope products and services rather than trying to solve for everything and everyone.

- Exercises can focus on evaluating the recovery of in-scope products and services using common disruptive event-related scenarios.

- Metrics can be developed that highlight the capabilities (and gaps) to recover in-scope products and services.

Chapter 32

Process:
Documented and Followed by All

A good program is based on clear, concise documentation that outlines methodology and the means to achieve continual improvement. The documentation needs to describe a clear process that must be followed by everyone in the organization who works to achieve value-adding and actionable business continuity outcomes. Let's begin with documentation and consider each element in turn.

Process documentation doesn't have to be complicated. In fact, it shouldn't be! Trapping people in overly complex flowcharts and technical jargon limits their interest in participating and, by extension, makes the business continuity professional's job more difficult.

You may be asking, what does documentation look like? In most organizations, it's composed of two documents or sets of documents:

1. A policy statement that succinctly summarizes management's business continuity expectations aligned to the style and content of other organizational policy statements. Typically, this statement is only a few pages, and often only one or two.

2. A list of SOPs that describe how the organization will meet the expectations stated in the policy and manage business continuity plans.

To produce a business continuity process that is followed by all, the documentation must be easy to find and written in a way that is understandable to non-business continuity professionals.

Our guidelines for process documentation are:

- Use bullets

- Write the 20 percent that addresses 80 percent of the process (80/20 rule)

- Include necessary information only; some areas will need details, but that doesn't mean everything does

- Ensure an outsider can understand it quickly

Here is sample content from a process document describing the BIA process:

- Program manager identifies the departments that support delivery of in-scope products and services, along with a department point of contact

- Program manager conducts interviews with the point of contact and subject matter experts to identify the following:

  ○ Activities that support product and service delivery

  ○ Resources required to perform key activities, including impact of the loss of these resources

  ○ Downtime tolerance based on in-scope product and service expectations

- Program manager or delegate documents the information gathered during the BIA interview

- Program manager or delegate sends BIA summary report to interviewees for feedback and approval (within seven days)

- Program manager summarizes results for all departments using the organization's BIA summary report template

- Program manager presents findings to the program sponsor and steering committee for feedback and approval

- ○ Key questions for the program sponsor and steering committee:
  - ✧ Is this the right picture?
  - ✧ Any changes to the in-scope list of products and services or downtime tolerances?

Once a process is documented, the challenge is getting everyone to follow it. This is particularly true in large organizations where the business continuity function extends beyond a program manager to include a team of people spread across the business. Challenging, yes; impossible, no!

The first step is to train everyone on the process. The best way to do this is to gather all the key program participants who will use this process together in a meeting, or series of meetings, and walk them through the process, literally reading the process out loud together. Once everyone has heard it, ask for questions. If something doesn't make sense to a participant, change it during the meeting. The goal is to walk out of that meeting with a process that everyone believes in and agrees to follow.

A walkthrough meeting is a great first step, but it alone will not result in a process that everyone follows. After the walkthrough meeting, it is the program manager's responsibility to ensure the process stays top of mind. Here are some ways to do that:

- Refer to the process regularly—keep it in people's minds

- Remember that the most common root causes of issues are the wrong people and the wrong process. When you think you have a 'wrong process' issue, display that process visually in a meeting so everyone can examine it and decide whether it needs to be changed.

- Be aware that processes naturally get more complex as the program grows. Every year or so, pick a process to renovate and simplify. This approach is a great way to push back against creeping complexity.

A program manager's discipline in using and updating the process is the main driver influencing whether it's followed by all.

Apply Methodology Effectively

With the BCOS, we chose not to focus primarily or exclusively on methodology but rather to solve the problems of program focus and engagement. Methodology details are well described by standards such as ISO 22301 and professional practices such as the BCI's GPG.

With that said, specific keys to success must be emphasized inside the standard methodology—because they are often overlooked. Be sure your process is covering these essentials:

Perform Analysis. Analysis is really made up of two parts: the BIA and the risk assessment. Don't get stuck here. Many people get lost in Analysis because there is so much data and they feel the need to identify, quantify, and justify everything right away. On top of that, risk assessment is a loaded concept. Google 'risk assessment' and you'll likely find thousands of ways to do it and just as many strong opinions. Our recommended approach when first implementing a risk assessment is to identify vulnerabilities to disruption and difficulties in recovering in a timely manner.

Keep the following tips in mind with the BIA and risk assessment to avoid 'analysis paralysis' so you can get to the Strategy phase as quickly as possible:

- Don't use a survey. You need to go and talk to people and help them understand what you're doing. As a bonus, you'll learn about the organization and build relationships during these interviews.

- Focus on understanding what activities and resources are needed to deliver in-scope products and services. For each activity, there are five types of resources to consider: facility (synonymous with workplace or premise), technology (including data), equipment, people, and supplier. Consider nonelectronic data and department/activity interdependencies as well.

- Start by capturing only resources that have a single point of failure, history of failure, or no easy alternatives (or alternatives with a long lead time to acquire). Gathering every resource that supports in-scope products and services can be overwhelming in some cases. For example, think of all the equipment needed in a hospital to provide trauma services—thousands of things! Start sensibly, and over time you can deepen the analysis if needed.

- Capture impacts to understand how downtime of a department and its activities impacts the organization, but don't fall into the analysis paralysis trap! Remember: the high-level requirements for downtime tolerances were set by the Frame Meeting participants as described in Chapter 31. As a result, you may need to gather some additional impact information during the BIA to aid in revising requirements and providing feedback to the steering committee's initial input.

- Once you have identified the resource dependencies, use the risk assessment to figure out how likely it is that a resource failure could result in product or service delivery failure and what you can do to limit the frequency of a disruption. This is where some estimate of likelihood of loss and impact of loss come into play. We rate the likelihood on a scale of one to ten, both for a disruption caused by the loss of the resource and for the impact to the organization. That way, we can quickly see where the highest-risk resources are. When we consider likelihood, we consider the controls in place that limit the resource loss. If you're interested in a risk assessment shortcut, especially in Year One, consider simply identifying resources that are single points of failure and difficult to recover in a timely manner. Odds are you'll find a lot to work on.

- As you might imagine, this is a lot of data. For most organizations, a software tool to manage this data is essential. Many are available; just search for 'business continuity software.'

Before moving to the Strategy phase of the BCOS, it's important to cover a topic that often introduces significant business continuity risk to just about any organization, that being third-party (aka supplier or vendor) risk. Many organizations choose to evaluate their most important vendors', suppliers', and business partners' business continuity programs and capabilities via the risk assessment process. In this case, importance means a third party that contributes to the delivery of in-scope products and services.

When engaging an in-scope third party:

- Assess single points of failure or other vulnerabilities related to the delivery of the product or service

- Determine whether the provider has a business continuity program in place (and if so, whether the program design is consistent with your expectations)

- Identify activity- and resource-specific recovery requirements and determine whether downtime tolerances are acceptable based on your product or service supported

- Review the results of any business continuity or IT disaster recovery testing initiatives relevant to the product or service provided

- Determine whether any portion of the product or service provided is subcontracted or outsourced to additional vendors, requiring further consideration

- Gather evidence of risk mitigation or program improvement activities for any deficiencies identified through the assessment process

- Assess supplier performance during actual incidents or disruptions

Along with these activities, review the contracts with your third parties to do the following:

- Identify any contractual language establishing business continuity or IT disaster recovery obligations for each in-scope third party

- Determine whether the contracts stipulate service-level agreements or clauses that guarantee levels of service in line with established recovery time objectives

- Determine whether force majeure language could limit supplier obligations during extraordinary events

Collectively, third-party-related residual risks—those outside of the organization's risk tolerance—should be addressed in the Strategy phase.

Determine Strategy. Once you know the activities and resources needed to deliver in-scope products and services, and the risks of losing them, the logical next step is to figure out what to do about those risks. That's where the Strategy phase comes in. **The goal here is to evaluate options to reduce the risk for key dependencies identified in the BIA. The strategy process includes both reducing the likelihood of losing a dependency (via protections, usually) and reducing the impact of losing a dependency (usually with backup sources or alternative processes).**

There are two ways to approach this:

- Determine general strategies that address a whole group of resource dependencies. For example, a work-from-home strategy may address many facility dependencies.

- Determine individual strategies that address a specific resource, such as a manual workaround when an application is down.

Not surprisingly, it works best to figure out general strategies first and then address anything that needs an individual continuity strategy. As you build these continuity strategies, you'll naturally identify a few critical areas that are tough to solve. These are the ones you should address with your steering committee's help.

When engaging the steering committee regarding continuity strategies, always provide options with broad cost implications. This approach will allow them to choose the best balance of risk and cost. Of course, one option always available is to do nothing—and that's okay. Just make sure the steering committee adjusts its product and service downtime tolerance accordingly.

During the Strategy phase, and prior to diving into documenting plans, it's important to identify which plans are needed and how their use will be coordinated by management following the onset of a disruption. We call this the response strategy. In most organizations, a crisis management plan serves as the overall umbrella process to manage the response and recovery effort. The next phase, Plans, dives deeper into planning.

Formulate Plans. When you've done the hard work of Analysis and Strategy, documenting plans gets a lot easier! Plans describe how to implement the strategies previously chosen.

Most plans answer three fundamental questions:

1. How do I, as the person using the plan, respond and recover using available strategies?

2. How do I, as the person responsible for a department, function, or activity, operate differently until returning to normal?

3. Who's involved in managing or participating in the response and recovery process?

Plans include answers to these questions, as well as other reference information that's often difficult to remember during a disaster.

There are many plan types, and organizations call them by different names (and some of the following plans may be managed and maintained in different parts of the organization):

- **Emergency response plans:** Describe the immediate response to a threat with the objective of protecting people and resources

- **Crisis management plans:** Outline more strategic responses to disruptive events with the objective of eliminating roadblocks to a timely recovery

- **Crisis communications plans:** Outline two-way methods to communicate and coordinate with different audiences to address concerns, protect reputations, and support response/recovery

- **Business continuity plans:** Describe how to continue or recover disrupted activities and resources with the objective of minimizing downtime and resuming the delivery of products and services

- **IT disaster recovery plans:** Guide the recovery of IT systems, applications, and services consistent with stakeholder expectations

Conduct Exercise. Exercises are critical because they serve as training tools for participants to learn about the response and recovery process, understand the stress of performing in a chaotic circumstance, and identify actions to improve the program. When building a program, it's important to start slowly with exercises to build the confidence of the team. The following list of exercises is in order, from least intense to most intense:

- **Seminar exercise** (or plan walkthrough): Exercise in which the participants are divided into groups to discuss specific issues

- **Tabletop exercise**: Facilitated exercise in which participants are given specific roles to perform, either as individuals or groups

- **Drill**: Coordinated, supervised activities usually employed to complete a single specific operation or procedure or function in a single process or department

- **Simulation**: Exercise in which a group of players, usually representing a control center or management team, react to a simulated incident notionally happening elsewhere

Once an exercise type is agreed upon, determine the scenario that will guide exercise participants and encourage them to use their business continuity plans. The following list provides some example scenarios:

- **Loss of facility**: Continuing the delivery of critical products and services following the loss of a key facility (e.g., fire)

- **Loss of people**: Continuing the delivery of critical products and services with a reduced workforce (e.g., pandemic)

- **Loss of technology**: Continuing the delivery of critical products and services without access to technology or systems (e.g., data center failure)

- **Loss of equipment**: Continuing the delivery of critical products and services following the loss of key equipment (e.g., metal press failure)

- **Loss of suppliers**: Continuing the delivery of critical products and services following the loss of key suppliers (e.g., payroll processing failure)

Immediately following an exercise, best practices include conducting a verbal debrief, after-action review, or 'hot wash' with participants to discuss immediate impressions and lessons learned. There are numerous other ways to solicit written feedback, including paper-based or internet surveys. Whether in-person or via survey, you'll get the best results using easy-to-answer questions with a ratings scale. Here are some sample questions:

- Describe your lessons learned, based on a review of the plans and the decisions made in response to the scenario.

- To what degree did the exercise meet your expectations?

- How satisfied were you with the overall time/duration of the exercise session?

- How do you rate the overall style and quality of the materials?

- How effectively did the facilitator present information?

- What are your recommendations for improvement, additional training needs, new topics, etc.?

Like a plan that sits unused on a shelf, exercise results that are documented but then ignored do little to improve response and recovery capabilities. As such, action items captured during the exercise should be entered in an issue log or actions list so that those items may be tracked to completion.

While exercise frequency requirements vary based on operating industry and standards, it's best to exercise business continuity plans and capabilities at least annually or following any significant organizational change.

Chapter 33

Participation:
Clear Roles, Right People

Building the right level of resilience requires having the right people contributing to the task. Many organizations suffer from poor program performance because they didn't ensure that key participants were the right fit for their roles.

It is common to see a business continuity program manager start working with people either assigned or available, with little thought as to whether people have the right skills, experiences, or empowerment for the assigned responsibilities. Strong program performance requires that the right people are associated with the right role.

Clear roles. Start by being clear about the different roles needed to achieve success and what you need from each role. Make a list of all the roles in the program, some of which you will have defined in the Frame Meeting. Then for each role, start a bulleted list of the role-specific requirements. This list should contain everything from the anticipated time commitment to knowledge of the business to responsibilities for updating plans. But keep the list focused on the most important things. We find most roles can be described in five to ten requirements. Here is an example:

Business Unit Business Continuity Coordinator

- Understands how the business unit contributes to in-scope products and services

- Drives the BIA documentation and plans continual improvement efforts

- Coordinates response activities for the business unit during an incident

- Leads business unit risk treatment

- Influences others through strong communication skills

- Demonstrates high proficiency with people skills and process-thinking

Once the role is clearly defined, it's simply a question of finding the right person to fill it.

Right people. At Castellan, when it comes time to clarify roles and responsibilities, we talk about 'GWC.' We learned of this three-letter acronym from the book *Traction* by Gino Wickman, who described a business operating model called the Entrepreneurial Operating System. The person assigned to each role should be able to respond positively to the following questions:

1. Do they ***get*** it (understand the role and responsibilities)?

2. Do they ***want*** it (motivated to take on the responsibility)?

3. Do they have the *capacity* to perform it (ability and time to perform the responsibilities)?

Gets it. This is a gut-feel type of question: does the person understand what the role is about and how it all comes together to help the organization? Do they see why it's important? For some people, this information just doesn't click.

Wants it. Does the person honestly want to do the job? Or is the person just going through the motions after being assigned to it? When you feel the need to motivate or energize a person in their role, that's a warning sign that the person just doesn't want to participate or do the work. In such cases, stop banging your head against the wall and find someone who wants it.

Has capacity. Does the person have the skills, resources, and time needed to perform the role well? Use the role definition you created to ask yourself whether the person has the mental capacity, the skills, and the time available to perform the role.

While *get it* and *want it* are mandatory, those who don't fully have the *capacity* for the role should still be considered if you believe they can develop the capacity with coaching or training in the next six months.

If you've been assigned people that you believe don't have GWC for the role, the following section is for you.

To rectify this situation, you *must* believe that you *do not* have to tolerate GWC issues in your program. Until you believe that, nothing will change. Even if it takes a year or more to fix, please know that you *can* have a program filled with people who get it, want it, and have the capacity to do the work. When that happens, *everything* gets easier.

So how should a program manager address GWC problems? First, always talk to the person one on one. During the conversation, you can ask whether the person gets it, wants it, and has the capacity for the role. Ninety percent of the time, the person knows there is a problem and will tell you all about it. Ten percent of the time, you'll need to help the person see your concerns. In either case, begin by talking to the person and getting on the same page that GWC is a problem.

Second, ask the person what the two of you should do about it. Often, the individual can find or suggest someone who is a better GWC fit, and you can move the program forward quickly. Sometimes, though, you just won't be able to find the right GWC fit. In these cases, you must add the problem to an issues list as a long-term problem to be monitored and addressed. In some cases, particularly for people with limited capacity, you can put in place workarounds that still allow the program to accomplish its goals. However, if no solutions can be found, present the issue to the steering committee to enlist their help in problem-solving. We'll cover how to do this in the following chapter.

Using clear roles and the GWC tool, over time, you *can* have a team composed of the right people to help achieve the right level of resilience.

Chapter 34

Engagement:
Frequency, Issues, Agendas

Business continuity succeeds only when participants engage with the program, but engagement isn't always easy. Engagement starts with compelling meetings that involve the right people on the right topics at the right time. It may sound simple, but you need your participants to participate!

One of the most important responsibilities of the business continuity program manager is to engage with others to design, build, and evolve the business continuity program. Your most important tool is effective meetings.

We've all sat through meetings where one person talks the whole time and no one even asks a question. It's boring, and it sucks the energy out of the room (literally or figuratively). At Castellan, to move the program forward and engage everyone in the process, we've designed a series of meetings, described in the table on the following page. Together, these meetings comprise the business continuity professional's engagement plan. You may choose to begin drafting the engagement plan at this point in the process or prior to the Frame Meeting (to help identify information requirements as part of the Frame Meeting's fourth question).

The Engagement Plan
The table on the following page suggests participants, frequency, and outcomes of each type of meeting. Avoid making changes to the meetings described in the table on the following page unless there is a strong business reason for doing so.

Core elements of the engagement plan include documenting and scheduling the following meetings:

What	Who	Frequency	Desired Outcome
Focus Meeting	Program manager and full-time team (core team)	Biweekly (every other week)	Build relationships, align on performance and resolve issues (brainstorming and decision-making)
Stakeholders Meeting	Those involved in planning and response (anyone who owns a plan)	Monthly	Build relationships, align on performance and on how to use plans
Management Review	Steering committee: operations, finance, IT, HR, audit/risk	Quarterly	Align on past program performance, identify goals for the quarter, and resolve issues (brainstorming and decision-making)
Annual Meeting	Steering committee and senior management	Annually	Same as above, but for the year ahead (this meeting replaces the fourth Quarterly Management Review)

Other interested parties, besides those listed in the table, exist in and around all organizations. Examples include boards of directors, auditors, customers, and other risk disciplines. Consult with each to determine the following:

1. Their motivation to engage (what you can offer them)

2. What they can offer to drive resiliency (what they can offer to the business continuity program)

3. How often they need to be engaged to add value

For each interested party grouping, define concrete outcomes and a plan to achieve each one. Add those to the engagement plan.

Focus Meeting

The Focus Meeting allows the core project team—typically people who are focused on business continuity full-time or nearly full-time—to maintain focus and clear priorities.

This meeting happens every two weeks with the core project team. Schedule sixty minutes for this meeting. The agenda and instructions follow.

Focus Meeting Agenda (60 minutes)

- Check-in (5 minutes)
- Scorecard (5 minutes)
- Quarterly goals (5 minutes)
- Actions (5 minutes)
- Issues resolution (35 minutes)
- Conclude (5 minutes)

Check-in. During check-in, go around the room and have everyone share some good news. For example, the best thing that has happened in their personal lives and the best thing that has happened at work since the previous meeting. The goal here is to begin focusing on each other and to connect personally.

Scorecard. The scorecard should highlight activity metrics that demonstrate that the team is moving forward effectively and making progress. The scorecard, discussed in detail in Chapter 35, is a summary of the current response and recovery capabilities of the organization, aligned to its in-scope products and services.

When reviewing the scorecard, the owner of each metric should read the number out loud and tell the group if it's on or off track. If the number is off track, add an issue to the issues list so it can be addressed by the team (discussed below) and move on. No discussing or solving at this point. This builds discipline and helps to ensure you're focusing on the most important thing. The scorecard review should take about five minutes.

Quarterly goals. Setting goals is covered in Chapter 36. For now, it's enough to say that goals should be reviewed at every meeting by asking one question: are we on- or off-track for achieving the goal? When a goal is off track, add an issue. Again, no discussing during this part of the meeting. This section should take only a few minutes.

Actions. Every Focus Meeting should result in a list of actions that need to be completed prior to the next meeting. During this part of the Focus Meeting, you should review the previous meeting's actions to ensure the action owner completed it. The program manager is responsible for the accountability of action completion. Agreeing to an action during a Focus Meeting is making a commitment to the team.

Issues. Most of the meeting should be focused on addressing issues (performance issues and opportunities for improvement). This is where the program manager has the biggest opportunity to move the program forward—and spending most of the meeting time addressing issues is the key to interesting meetings! Issue processing should be dynamic and involve everyone. Examples of issues that need to be addressed include a high percentage of expired business continuity plans, poor turnout for business continuity awareness training, or minimal attendance during Quarterly Management Reviews.

Keep a list of issues for the team in a central place and add to it as you go through the beginning part of the Focus Meeting. When you're ready to start addressing issues, confirm with the team that the issues list is complete, and then quickly identify the top three issues that, if solved, would move the program forward. Most teams just yell out what they want to talk about.

Once you've identified your top three issues, start working on the first one. Sometimes issues are easy to solve and take only a few minutes; sometimes they take more than one meeting. If you work them in priority order, the key is to solve them effectively (i.e., solve them permanently) and identify an action to address the root cause.

Issues typically fall into three categories:

1. A problem that needs a solution

2. A topic that needs to be communicated

3. A recommendation or an idea that needs brainstorming or approval

The key to solving problems forever is to solve them at the root cause level. We call that diagnosing. Luckily, as part of the BCOS, diagnosing is straightforward. We have found there are only seven root causes (the seven components of the BCOS wheel):

1. Frame

2. Process

3. Participation

4. Engagement

5. Measurables

6. Improvement

7. Automation

When diagnosing, just ask yourself: which of these is the real root cause of the problem? Then solve for that. This book is full of tools to address these root causes.

Once you've diagnosed and found the real problem to fix, you can discuss potential solutions. But before identifying solutions, look at the problem from different angles and get everyone involved. Encourage the meeting participants to ask lots of questions until there are none left to ask! Then confirm you're still working on the real problem.

If so, then start brainstorming solutions. When the brainstorming runs out of steam, someone needs to make a decision. Start by confirming that the issue remains *the* core issue, then suggest a solution. Capture whatever needs to happen next with an action item. The outcomes of issue processing are *actions*, each of which is assigned to an owner with a due date. Examples of actions include communicating the outcomes of the discussion to a specified audience, making a change to program documentation, and escalating the issue to another meeting for resolution.

Conclude. Spend the last five minutes reviewing new actions and rating the meeting using a one-to-ten scale. Anyone rating the meeting a seven or lower should explain why and consider adding the reason to the issues list for next time.

Stakeholder Meeting

For larger organizations where you might have appointed part-time coordinators in major lines of business or business units, a sixty-minute Monthly Stakeholder Meeting focuses on sharing knowledge (what's working that everyone should know about) and issue processing.

Stakeholder Meeting Agenda (60 minutes)
• Scorecard (5 minutes)
• Actions (5 minutes)
• Training (20 minutes)
• Issues (25 minutes)
• Conclude (5 minutes)

Scorecard. The scorecard for the Stakeholder Meeting should focus on activity metrics for which stakeholders are responsible. These metrics are often BIA and plan completion rates. See Chapter 35 for more details. Remember to limit discussion during the scorecard review to on-track or off-track. Add anything that is off-track to the issues list.

Actions. As in the Focus Meeting, the group should review previous actions to hold every person accountable for delivering on his or her commitments.

Training. Spend this time taking a deep dive on something relevant to the stakeholders. For example, before refreshing the BIA, consider holding training on the BIA that month. Alternatively, the training may involve taking a deeper look at how the organization manages the response to a disruption and how all the departments feed into the response effort. The key here is to be creative in choosing both the topic and how it's presented. A training with a PowerPoint and one person talking the whole time is boring, so mix it up. Get participants talking any way you can. For example, consider an activity or a quiz with a discussion following. Better yet, get a participant to deliver training or make a presentation on something that's working well.

Issues. During a Stakeholder Meeting, follow the same process for dealing with issues as in the Focus Meeting, but with ones that are relevant to this stakeholder group. The goal here is to get the participants to identify issues. *If the stakeholders are not contributing, they aren't engaged.*

The easiest way to mine for issues is to facilitate the following exercise:

- Have everyone take a few quiet minutes to write down what's working and not working with the business continuity program.

- Go around the room and ask everyone to share their answers.

- Add everything that isn't working as an issue. If something that's working for one participant could help others, make that an issue too.

Conclude. As in the Focus Meeting, spend the last five minutes reviewing new actions and rating the meeting. Anyone who rates the meeting a seven or lower should explain why.

Quarterly Management Review

Once per quarter is a good frequency to reengage with management, often via the steering committee, to demonstrate progress, ensure the program is meeting expectations, and remain aligned to the organization's strategy.

Once per quarter, cover the following topics with the steering committee. Schedule sixty minutes for this meeting.

Quarterly Management Review Agenda (60 minutes)
• Previous quarterly goals (5 minutes)
• Scorecard (5 minutes)
• Key risks, high-impact actions, and issues (30 minutes)
• New quarterly goals (3–5) (10 minutes)
• Conclude (10 minutes)

Previous quarterly goals. Use this time to review the previous quarter and hold yourself accountable for either achieving or not achieving the quarterly goals. Talk about any lessons learned from the quarter, then close the books and start looking forward to the next quarter.

Product and service scorecard. Spend this time reviewing the product and service scorecard with the steering committee. If there are issues, add them to the issues list at the end (if they aren't already there). Details for setting up the scorecard as a dashboard are in Chapter 35.

Major open risks, high-impact actions, other issues. As with the Focus Meeting, the largest portion of the meeting should engage participants in processing issues. Keep any major risks or high-impact actions on the list of issues for visibility to the steering committee. Consider using some of the time for special topics, such as discussing changes to the planning process, how this group should be notified of a disruption, and how the group should be pulled into the response of a disruption. Let the steering committee identify what they want to work on, but guide them toward large budgetary items, customer-facing issues, and unresolved strategic issues that could have a significant impact if left unresolved. Some organizations choose to use some of this time to discuss emerging risks or recent disruptions affecting others.

Note: Any issues or risks that will be addressed in a new quarterly goal can be removed from the list.

New quarterly goals. When setting new quarterly goals, we suggest bringing three to five proposed goals and engaging the steering committee to discuss whether they are the right goals. Warning: if you present your goals and everyone nods and you move on, you're missing the purpose of the exercise. Each goal is a discussion point. If you're struggling to get everyone to engage, create a requirement that every participant must identify one goal he or she would remove. Or ask each steering committee member to identify a program goal he or she would be willing to sponsor. Examples of program-level goals include 1) expand the program scope to include a new business acquisition and 2) select a new call center recovery strategy to drive 30 percent cost savings.

Conclude. As in the Focus Meeting, spend the last five minutes reviewing new actions and rating the meeting. Anyone who rates the meeting a seven or lower should be asked to explain why.

Annual Meeting

The BCOS includes an Annual Meeting for two reasons: 1) business continuity steering committees are seldom composed of the most senior leaders in an organization and 2) some industries require annual business continuity presentations to boards of directors. More strategic than the Quarterly Management Reviews, this annual session focuses on performance review, review of annual goals, and higher-level issue processing.

Note: The Annual Meeting can replace the fourth Quarterly Management Review in most organizations.

Annual Meeting Agenda (60 minutes)
• Program summary review (15 minutes)
• Product and service dashboard (10 minutes)
• Key risks, high-impact actions, and issues (20 minutes)
• New annual + quarterly goals (10 minutes)
• Conclude (5 minutes)

Program summary review. This is an opportunity to review the four questions from the Frame Meeting to ensure leadership is still on the same page about the direction of the program. For each question, read the previously agreed upon answer and ask whether this answer still applies. If it does, move on. If not, decide whether the question needs to be addressed right then or added to the issues list.

Product and service dashboard. The setup of this dashboard is covered in Chapter 35. Use this time to review it with the leadership team. If there are any issues, add them to the issues list.

Key risks, high-impact actions, and issues. This portion of the meeting should work like issue processing in the Management Review Meeting. Let the leadership team identify what they want to work on solving—and drive the group to solve it forever, using the issues processing guidance above.

New annual + quarterly goals. As with the Management Review Meeting, bring three to five proposed goals and engage leadership in a discussion, which is the objective for this part of the agenda.

Get Uncomfortable

BCOS meetings should be one or more of the following:

- Fun
- Intense
- Interesting
- Surprising
- Uncomfortable

These are the types of words we might use to describe a movie we enjoy. That's what engagement looks like. If you want great engagement, be willing to enter the danger zone and take some risks.

One rule of thumb we use at Castellan: the most important issue to talk about is the one that scares the meeting participants the most. That's how you know you're getting close to the most impactful and game-changing issue that needs to be solved to move forward.

If your meetings do not have some of the emotions above, ask the group why and process that as an issue.

Chapter 35

Measurables:
Products, Services, Activities, Compliance

Before diving into the measurables included in BCOS, let's look at why measurables are essential to achieving the right level of resilience. There are five core reasons:

1. **Answer fundamental questions about program performance.** Metrics help answer core questions, such as 'Can we recover?' Metrics help tell a story and deliver meaningful insight to those seeking to understand why the program exists and what capabilities are in place.

2. **Effect change.** To effectively communicate the need to alter a program's current course of action, a program manager must have the measurables to justify the program's position. Having this information is especially critical if that change requires an increase in resources. The ability to highlight less-than-optimal performance and drill down to the root cause is paramount in initiating, leading, and managing change.

3. **Drive continual improvement.** Effective metrics don't just tell a story, they also paint a picture for the future. Metrics provide a window into the organization's existing shortfalls and gaps. They can be used to highlight those areas that either have been improved or need to be improved.

4. **Drive action.** 'What gets measured gets done.' While the origin of this quote is debated, the truth behind it is not. Good metrics help paint a picture of what work has been done and what still needs to be done.

5. **Meet requirements.** Every modern standard and regulatory requirement cite the use of metrics to drive program performance. If you desire to align or comply with any of a myriad of standards, you will be required to have measurables. So you might as well have good measurables!

BCOS has two types of metrics: Activity + Compliance Metrics and Product + Service Metrics.

Activity + Compliance Metrics

These are straightforward metrics that ensure that program deliverables and outcomes are on track and consistent with expectations. Chances are you already track some of these, including the number of BIAs updated, number of plans updated, and/or number of exercises completed. Activity and compliance metrics help answer the question, 'Are we doing what we said we would (or should) do?'

Activity metrics track the completion of key deliverables in the business continuity lifecycle. Often, regulatory or customer requirements outline the need for specific program elements. By completing these *activities* and tracking their progress, the program manager can monitor and report on the organization's progress toward achieving *compliance* with the requirements. These items also demonstrate what work has been performed to date and what still needs to be executed in comparison to requirements, both internal and external.

Activity and compliance metrics should answer the question, 'Is everyone involved with the program doing what they are supposed to?' Here are some examples of activity and compliance metrics:

- Number of BIAs completed or updated compared to total expected

- Number of supplier business continuity assessments completed compared to total in-scope suppliers

- Number of tabletop exercises conducted and post-exercise reports produced and approved

There are two key audiences for activity and compliance metrics:

Core business continuity team. Every member of this group should have an activity metric that he or she is responsible for and empowered to drive. These metrics are reviewed every two weeks during the Focus Meeting.

Stakeholders. Each stakeholder should also have metrics that are relevant to their area and their responsibilities. These metrics are reviewed monthly during the Stakeholder Meeting.

Most business continuity software packages do a great job of tracking activity metrics. Here's an example:

Department	BIA	Plan	Capability	Exercise	Overall
Accounts Payable	100	100	100	100	100
Accounts Receivable	100	100	100	0	75
Analytics	100	100	100	0	75
Architecture	100	100	100	0	75
Automobile Claims	50	0	50	0	25

Product + Service Metrics

These metrics help program leaders focus on evaluating the actual recoverability of the business activities and resources that contribute to the delivery of the in-scope products and services. Product and service metrics are an essential yet often overlooked part of the business continuity performance measurement process. The reason is simple: activity and compliance metrics are *boring* to executives and customers because their questions can't be answered with metrics that focus on 'doing a business continuity planning task.' They seek to answer the following questions:

- What is our ability to deal with business interruptions? (Or what level of resiliency do we really have to address product and service continuity?)

- What is our confidence level in our capabilities?

- Where are the remaining gaps and risks?

As you can see, these questions can't be answered with BIA approval statistics. So how can you build metrics to answer what executives really want to know? The answer is deceptively simple.

It starts with the products and services identified in the Frame Meeting. The executives told you what is important to them, and they even told you their tolerance for downtime.

Now, you need to tell them about the organization's ability to meet those targets—*on one page*.

The table below provides an example of this metric that shows executive leadership the capability of the program. Of course, much of the information is not presented here, but that's the point—this is a high-level performance summary. Your BIA and business continuity strategy selection process should generate all the data needed to populate a table like this:

Product / Service / Business Process	Business Continuity Objective	Current State Recovery Capability	Rating
Perform customer support	Ensure no more than four hours' downtime with less than a ninety- second wait time	Eight hours, estimated sixty-second wait time at recovery	◯ Ⓨ ◯
Manufacture product	Ensure ten days' target safety stock (offsite), maintain contingency sourcing agreement effective within seven days	One day's safety stock, contingency sourcing agreement with Acme pending	Ⓡ ◯ ◯
Process warranty claims	Provide for seamless failover between each claims-handling region in the United States	Claims failover process complete and demonstrated no downtime	◯ ◯ Ⓖ

Product / Service / Business Process	Business Continuity Objective	Current State Recovery Capability	Rating
Bill customers	Restart bill generation and catch up on all backlogged work within five days, suspend collection reminders to protect customer relationship	Billing tested and restarted in three days, backlog closed in four days	⚪⚪Ⓖ

In this case, red (R) means a lack of alignment to expectations, yellow (Y) means a partial alignment with the organization and heading in the right direction, and green (G) means alignment is currently in place.

In the example shown, two of the metrics are red or yellow. When a metric highlights a problem or missed expectations, the program manager needs to be prepared to discuss why and include a root-cause analysis. This discussion should be processed as an issue, leading to a solution to get to green.

How to Determine 'Good' Metrics

You may wonder how we will know whether the metrics we've developed are good, To find out, examine your scorecard and then ask yourself the following questions:

1. Are you highlighting your recovery capabilities (and gaps) compared to your business continuity requirements?

2. Are you doing what you should to prepare (based on input provided during the Frame Meeting and your process documentation)?

3. Do your interested parties feel informed to help drive continual improvement?

If you can answer yes to those three questions, chances are you've developed metrics that matter. But if you're still struggling to develop good metrics or a good scorecard for a specific group of people (such as Focus Meeting participants), consider these points:

1. Scorecards are an incredibly useful tool. The objective of the scorecard is to determine whether the program is on track in achieving the right level of resilience.

2. For every team's scorecard, identify five to ten measures that help participants understand the performance of the program or program activities and whether the outcomes they contribute to are tracking with expectations.

   a. In a group discussion with all Focus Meeting participants about creating the scorecard, you could pose this question in a broad, programmatic way: 'What are all the foundational measurables to predict business continuity success?' Then pare the list down to the critical few.

   b. In a one-on-one conversation with a member of the team that participates in a Focus Meeting, you may ask, 'What are the key measurables that you own based on your responsibilities? What are the key measurables for someone else, especially if it contributes to your success?' If you choose this path, you may want to summarize all the nominations and review with the team leader or process them as an issue to come up with the critical few.

3. The measurables should be quantitative, if possible. For each measurable, have a performance target in mind. That way, when the team members meet, they can determine whether the program is on track and, if not, create an issue and process it.

4. Some measurables don't move daily, weekly, or even monthly. Therefore, it might not make sense to talk about them during every meeting. Some could be reviewed once a month or even quarterly.

5. Assign an owner for each scorecard item. Each owner should be prepared to state whether the item is on- or off-track during each meeting.

6. The optimal number of scorecard items for each meeting will vary. But be sure to get to the core foundational issues that lead to achieving the right level of resilience.

7. As you develop a scorecard, remember that every meeting participant should contribute to the number on that scorecard!

One last reminder: good scorecards alone won't guarantee success. A momentum killer is introducing and reviewing metrics but not working to solve the root causes of consistently missed targets. Remember, there are only seven root causes as highlighted in Chapter 34: Frame, Process, Participation, Engagement, Measurables, Improvement, and Automation.

Chapter 36

Improvement:
Goals, Actions, and Experiments

Why is improvement important? American writer William S. Burroughs once stated, "When you stop growing, you start dying." This is true of any endeavor, including BCOS.

For some organizations, the tools for improvement are less about getting better and more about managing an overwhelming amount of work to be done. If you're at an organization that just has *so much* to do to achieve the right level of resilience, it can be overwhelming. The tools below will help you compartmentalize things so you can focus on what's important now and communicate clearly what the long-term vision looks like.

Here is how we do that at Castellan:

Most improvement items start out as an issue—either through discussions with executives or by completing business continuity planning activities, such as the risk assessment or during the selection of a strategy. But the key to the picture above is to put each topic in *only* one box at any given time. As you're processing issues, push things to the right until they're achievable during that time period. Then focus on the areas to the left that you can address now. When you use this process with executives, they will begin to understand what is achievable and what is not, given the current resources allocated to the program.

The inverse is also true. For the 'big ticket' items that require significant time to address, work backward and identify the work that needs to be done to prepare for the longer-term goal.

Let's take a closer look at actions, experiments, and goals.

Actions and Experiments

Actions

Actions are improvement opportunities that can be addressed over the short term. While actions are often the result of exercises or real-life incidents, they can come from any stage of the business continuity planning lifecycle. Actions are used to hold individuals accountable and provide specific steps to mature the program.

Great actions have the following elements:

- A specific outcome
- One owner (multiple owners is a common reason for actions not being addressed)
- A project plan or roadmap describing how to realize the desired outcome
- A due date
- A process for follow-up when complete

Actions are primarily used in the context of Focus, Stakeholder, and Management Review Meetings, where owners of a newly created action can commit to completing the action by the due date.

Here's an example of an action that's specific to one in-scope department:

Implement a facility recovery strategy for the payroll department based on the management-approved recovery time objective of thirty-six hours.

Here's another example of an action that might be program-specific and reviewed during a Focus Meeting:

Achieve full compliance with our exercise standards, as documented in our SOP, by planning for, facilitating, and reporting on the three remaining department-level tabletop exercises by the first of next month.

The standard due date for actions coming out of one of these meetings is the next time the meeting occurs, but some actions clearly take more than one or two weeks. This approach to action completion focuses on accountability.

Experiments

Experiments are a special type of action. They must be low-risk actions where failure is always an option and the primary goal is learning.

Experiments are sometimes strategic and sometimes tactical, but the goal is always to try new things in a controlled environment so you can determine whether something new might help the organization better treat risk. For example, you might work with your IT team to attempt an application failover at an alternative site or have a team work remotely one day per month to determine what they might miss if they could not access the facility. In either of these cases, the emphasis should be about learning rather than success or failure.

There are two major types of experiments: program experiments and strategy experiments.

Program experiments. These experiments are trials designed to enhance how a program operates. Examples include the following:

- Allowing departments to facilitate exercises on their own
- Developing short checklist plans instead of longer manuals

Strategy experiments. These experiments are designed to test potential strategies before fully implementing them. Examples include the following:

- Trying open-source mass notification tools (e.g., WhatsApp) for crisis communications

- Having a group work from home

Goals: Quarterly, 1-Year, and 3-Year

Business continuity program goals help drive long-term growth and maturation. Without goals, it can be difficult for the program manager to guide a program, and other program stakeholders will not have an aligned end-state or vision for the program itself. To achieve this vision, three sets of goals help drive the program forward: quarterly, annual, and three-year. As a best practice, the goals should cascade from the three-year to the annual to the quarterly goals (with quarterly goals helping to achieve the annual goals and the annual goals contributing to the achievement of three-year goals).

When setting goals, ensure that each goal aligns with the organization's strategic values by enlisting the input of the steering committee and other senior leaders. Update goals during ongoing Quarterly and Annual Management Review Meetings.

Let's talk more about quarterly goal setting for a moment. This is one of the most important tasks for members of a Focus Meeting (in other words, the full-time equivalents in an organization focused on business continuity). Here are a couple of thoughts when setting these goals:

1. These are quarterly goals, so clearly state the completion date (the goal must be complete by January 15, 20XX).

2. As a team, start by setting the one to three most important things the team needs to accomplish this quarter to achieve the right level of resilience.

3. Assign an owner to each goal.

4. Revise the wording to make each goal 'SMART:'

   a. **Specific:** goals are clear and well-defined

   b. **Measurable:** goal success can be measured

   c. **Attainable:** goals are achievable

    d. **Relevant:** goals resonate with priorities

    e. **Time-bound:** goals have a deadline

5. Give the owner of each goal an action to build a plan for achieving the goal. The action plan can be simple, but it needs to provide clarity to the team on what, when, and who will be needed.

Chapter 37

Automation:
Digitize and Recommend

Years ago, when I first entered the business continuity profession, I used to suggest that business continuity software was valuable but not essential.

Things have changed.

I can't remember the last time I offered feedback to a client that software was a nice-to-have.

Organizations are more complex than ever and face an ever-increasing threat landscape.

Without making a commercial endorsement of any kind, organizations leveraging business continuity software achieve higher levels of readiness for disruption with fewer resources, and they are more effective in deploying a timely, more informed response.

While there are many options on the market, business continuity software should essentially deliver three core outcomes:

1. **Integration:** connects to the essential sources of organizational information, internal and external, that enable the digitization of the environment in which they operate

2. **Intelligence:** the digitization effort should enable an organizational ability to predict disruption, highlight areas of noncompliance, and effectively respond to and recover from a disruption in the timeliest manner possible

3. **Automation:** moves work that doesn't require 'reasoning' to software, freeing program participants to solve problems, close issues, and improve response/recovery capabilities

When realizing these three core outcomes, organizations that invest in business continuity software gain the ability to do the following:

1. Identify vulnerabilities that could lead to an increased frequency of disruption (which results in a decreased frequency of disruption)

2. Determine appropriate business continuity requirements, taking into account a wide range of influencers, obligations, and interdependencies

3. Understand each critical path that contributes to the delivery of essential products and services

4. Identify the implications associated with the disruption, specifically how the loss of availability of activities and resources affects products/services, which helps inform and structure a better, more focused response

All in all, business continuity software delivers efficiency, but more importantly, it helps you cut through the noise to identify vulnerabilities that could disrupt the execution of the organization's strategy.

At this point, we have worked our way through the seven core components of the BCOS model: Frame, Process, Participation, Engagement, Measurables, Improvement, and Automation. If you have a problem in your business continuity program, we're confident you can trace it back to one of these sources. Now it's time to put it all together into a new or existing program. The following chapter explains how we at Castellan approach implementing a BCOS program.

Chapter 38

Putting It All Together

At Castellan, most of our consulting work is focused on implementing BCOS, either when building a program from the ground up or applying it to an existing program. In either case, the structure is the same. Over time, we made sure each of our clients' business continuity programs had the seven core components in the wheel by applying an approach composed of six phases: Startup, Analysis, Strategy, Plans, Exercise, and Improve. As you'll see, this structure aligns with Michael's journey as he worked to create the right level of resilience for Felder.

This chapter explains our proven method of implementation and why it works.

Phase 1: Startup

Although the title may imply starting from the beginning or starting over or that this phase applies only to an organization without a business continuity program, none of those are true. Even for our clients with mature business continuity programs, it's useful to consider reviewing and deploying the five tools and processes that are part of Startup (and refreshing the results over time as well). These steps are frame the program, develop an engagement plan, get the right people, specify the process to be followed by all (FBA), and resolve issues.

Frame the program. Not surprising, one of the first activities to be completed is the Frame Meeting, because everything flows from there. The four Frame Questions, and the discussion that takes place with each, set the foundation for focus and engagement. (For more on the Frame process, see Chapter 31 and be sure to visit castellanbc.com/felder for a Frame Meeting recording.)

Develop an engagement plan. The engagement plan is one of the first tools developed and used following the Frame Meeting. This document summarizes the long-term engagement model that the organization plans to use to engage all program participants and key stakeholders. (For more on the engagement plan, see Chapter 34.)

Get the right people. During Startup, we work to identify or confirm the people who occupy key business continuity program roles. The Frame Meeting helps identify key roles, and the engagement plan outlines the methods of long-term interaction. The time to confirm the specific people who GWC (get it, want it, and have capacity) is during Startup. Issues with the right people should be solved as early as possible to gain momentum for the program. (For more on the topic of identifying the right people, see Chapter 33.)

Specify the process FBA. FBA stands for 'followed by all.' Throughout this book, we talk about setting and sharing expectations for the business continuity program and planning process with all participants. Startup is the right time to begin documenting your process. As you go through your planning lifecycle, you may change the process—and that's *good*! A process document should be a living tool, referenced and updated regularly. Start that habit at the beginning. (For more on process documentation, see Chapter 32.)

Resolve issues. We introduce the topic of issue processing in Startup for one important reason. Even for organizations brand new to business continuity who are implementing a best-in-class business continuity program for the first time, challenges will emerge. It's important to tackle design and execution problems head-on with a strong approach to get to the root cause of the issue. (For more on issue processing, see Chapter 34.)

Phase 2: Analysis

The Frame process helps define the program scope at the product and service level. Analysis helps define business continuity requirements for activities and resources, as well as risk mitigation opportunities that help to decrease the frequency or impact of disruption. These activities are collectively known as the BIA and risk assessment. (For more on the BIA and risk assessment, see Chapter 32, ISO 22317, and ISO 31000).

One-hour interviews & five dependencies. The BIA involves data gathering interviews with individual departments or functions to better understand how the organization performs its business activities, and if disrupted, the impact on in-scope products and services. We find that one hour is usually enough for these interviews.

During these discussions, it's important to identify the five resource dependencies that activities use to create value: people, facility, equipment, information technology (and data), and suppliers, as well as other information needs and interdependencies. With these dependencies, Castellan seeks to understand single points of failure, vulnerability to disruption, and any difficulty in replacing resources if lost.

Activity metrics. During Analysis activity, you can begin measuring program performance. This starts with monitoring completion rate of BIAs to drive execution. As additional program activities are started, such as planning and exercising, add those to the activity metrics and review the results of this level of measurement during recurring Focus Meetings.

Phase 3: Strategy

Why perform business continuity planning unless you pursue methods to limit business continuity risk? The Strategy phase involves *identifying options* to mitigate business continuity risk, *choosing* the options that best meet the organization's needs, and then *implementing* (and maintaining) the solutions so they are available prior to the onset of a disruptive event.

Once strategy options are chosen, it's time to build product and service metrics based on those choices. Be sure to share this information during Quarterly Management Review Meetings.

For more on the Strategy identification, selection, and implementation process, see Chapter 32 (as well as ISO 22331). And for more information on product/service metrics, see Chapter 35.

Phase 4: Plans

As Michael discovered early in his business continuity planning assignment, as important as plans are, they are just one outcome of the business continuity planning process. In general, plans describe how to respond to and recover from a disruption. There are many different types of plans, and although the names may vary by organization, the most common plan types include the following:

- **Crisis management:** Describes how the organization will manage the strategic response to the disruption

- **Crisis communications:** Describes how the organization will maintain two-way communication with key stakeholders throughout the disruptive event

- **Emergency response:** Describes how the organization will manage the immediate response to preserve life and property

- **Business continuity:** Describes how the organization will continue essential activities and recover as quickly as possible, consistent with expectations

- **IT disaster recovery:** Describes how the organization will recover IT assets and services

Regardless of type, a good plan has these key characteristics:

- Clear communication and guidance

- Clear roles, responsibilities, and assignments

- Clearly defined recovery steps (how to recover)

- Concise and manageable content

- Summarized 'reference content' (to help readers remember)

When developing and documenting your plan, **avoid** these common pitfalls:

- **Bloated:** The plan contains unnecessary detail or extra content that's not needed when responding to a disruptive event

- **Templatized:** Rather than describing how to recover, the plan contains boilerplate content that isn't distinguishable from other business areas

- **Inappropriately focused:** Content is about responding to threats rather than the recovery of the business following a loss of resources

Also make sure the plan is accessible—that people know where to get a copy of the plan when it's needed.

For more on the Plans phase, see Chapter 32 (and ISO 22332).

Phase 5: Exercise

The focus of the Exercise phase is to make business continuity planning 'real' for everyone in the organization. This effort includes creating business continuity awareness for all employees (outside of Exercise sessions) and exercises for those who will be involved in the response and recovery effort.

Employee awareness initiatives focus on the overall structure of the program, employee responsibilities during a disruptive event, and what employees can expect for communications.

Exercises usually start out basic (such as walking through the plan) but then should evolve to navigating challenging real-life scenarios. Extensive guidance on exercises is available in ISO 22398 and ISO 22313.

In addition to ISO-level guidance, our focus is on giving planning participants some realistic events that create 'muscle memory.' We've found this is the most memorable training—and when you need people to remember what to do during a disaster, memorable is important.

Phase 6: Improve

Once a full planning lifecycle has been completed, it's time to transition the focus to the long-term operation of the program. The Improve phase involves the tools and meeting cadence needed for long-term success.

During this phase, it's important to continue implementing the Biweekly Focus Meetings, Monthly Stakeholder Meetings, Quarterly Management Review Meetings with the steering committee, and Annual Meeting. This meeting cadence ensures program alignment with the organization's strategy and priorities and addresses any issues that are impeding progress. The steering committee-level engagement includes reviewing product and service metrics and the progress of any strategy implementation projects.

At the Improve phase, it is time to begin tracking quarterly, annual, and three-year goals, as described in Chapter 36.

At Castellan, we've developed a Check It tool to be used annually to confirm that the organization continues to strengthen its alignment to BCOS. The full Check It tool is in Chapter 39. In addition to this approach to self-assess alignment with the BCOS, we recommend you request independent program assessments from an internal audit department or a qualified third party.

This is the process we use at Castellan to implement the BCOS with our clients throughout the world! Or more accurately, this is our targeted starting point that we adjust based on unique circumstances. While you can use whatever process works best for you, many of these components reinforce one another. We strongly suggest using them together.

Chapter 39

Check It

The Check It tool is designed to help measure your organization's alignment to the BCOS and identify actions to drive further alignment. This tool is not a one-use effort. Rather, consider using it annually to measure progress and continual improvement (and it serves as a great source of issue identification). We also encourage involving key program stakeholders in data gathering as well as in results discussions. Internally at Castellan, we consider an organization aligned to the BCOS model only when it scores 80 percent or higher on the assessment, which essentially measures alignment to the seven core components of the BCOS. Chapters 30 to 37 offer input on how to raise your score!

For each question, score your program on a scale of 1 (strongly disagree) to 4 (strongly agree) and then add up the results.

1. Our organization uses automation (software and other tools) to accomplish regular recurring tasks, enabling the program manager/team to focus on program improvement rather than administrative tasks.   1   2   3   4

2. Our organization uses automation (software or other tools) to manage business continuity incidents.   1   2   3   4

3. The program manager uses automation to analyze   1   2   3   4
   program performance and provide insights into
   where the program may have gaps.

4. Our core business continuity team (full-time resources   1   2   3   4
   leading the program) connects regularly to discuss
   and solve issues that move the program forward.

5. Our business continuity program is well integrated   1   2   3   4
   with other risk disciplines within the organization
   (e.g., information security, emergency/incident
   response, IT disaster recovery).

6. Our process (department or function) level business   1   2   3   4
   continuity representatives meet regularly to be trained
   in their responsibilities as well as solve issues that limit
   their effectiveness.

7. Our organization understands why it has invested in   1   2   3   4
   a business continuity program, which is documented
   and understood by all.

8. Our senior management agrees on the products and   1   2   3   4
   services the business continuity program is working to
   protect and the maximum downtime tolerance for each.

9. Our core business continuity team seeks feedback on   1   2   3   4
   improvement opportunities and establishes quarterly
   goals that help drive us toward the right level of resilience.

10. The program can effectively improve and adapt to the   1   2   3   4
    organization's changing business strategy and is
    appropriately funded to enable approved strategies,
    risk mitigation controls, and other improvement
    opportunities.

11. Our organization tracks and follows up on the status   1 2 3 4
    of to-dos, action items, and experiments to ensure
    accountability.

12. Our organization tracks and reviews the completion   1 2 3 4
    rate for business continuity planning activities,
    such as plan updates and exercises.

13. Senior management regularly reviews our ability to   1 2 3 4
    recover in-scope products and services.

14. We have documented our business continuity program   1 2 3 4
    roles and responsibilities.

15. Everyone with a role in our business continuity   1 2 3 4
    program understands expectations, wants to participate
    in their role, and has the capacity (time and knowledge)
    needed to execute their role well.

16. Senior management decision-makers (referred to as a   1 2 3 4
    crisis management team) are ready to convene quickly
    to coordinate an efficient response to a disruption.

17. Our employees are aware of their roles in responding   1 2 3 4
    to and recovering from a disruption.

18. Our organization has a cross-functional steering   1 2 3 4
    committee that meets regularly to review the
    recoverability of in-scope products and services,
    prioritize corrective actions, and address strategic
    issues that may be impeding our ability to achieve
    the right level of resilience.

19. Our organization has a process for how we perform   1 2 3 4
    business continuity activities, which is documented,
    simple and straightforward, and followed by all
    program participants.

20. Our organization mapped in-scope products and   1   2   3   4
    services to their underlying activity dependencies
    (facilities, technologies, equipment, people, and
    suppliers), and all have downtime tolerances.

21. Our organization has selected recovery strategies for   1   2   3   4
    in-scope product/service dependencies, consistent
    with our risk tolerance.

22. Our business continuity plans include actionable   1   2   3   4
    content that describes what needs to be recovered,
    by whom, how it will be recovered, and when the
    plans should be used.

23. Our organization conducts exercises to demonstrate   1   2   3   4
    an ability to respond to disruptions and recover our
    in-scope products and services.

24. Our organization has a protocol for how response   1   2   3   4
    participants (from employees to senior management)
    communicate during a disruption and everyone is
    trained on it.

25. Our organization conducts regular training and   1   2   3   4
    awareness activities to ensure everyone in the
    organization is aware of the business continuity
    program and their role in response to and recovery
    from disruptions.

You may be wondering which questions map to each BCOS component. While some questions relate to multiple components, the following table maps each question only to the component that is most closely aligned with:

Component	Question Mapping
Frame	7, 8
Process	19, 20, 21, 22, 23, 24, 25
Participation	14, 15, 16, 17, 18
Engagement	4, 5, 6
Measurables	12, 13
Improvement	9, 10, 11
Automation	1, 2, 3

Chapter 40

Two Points of Clarification

Throughout the Felder fable, two terms were used often: 'crisis management' and 'IT disaster recovery.'

Yet we often collectively summarized the different preparedness/readiness processes and outcomes using the term 'business continuity.'

So what's the real difference, and how do the three relate?

Let's start with revisiting the definition of business continuity from the book's preface.

Business continuity is all about trying to keep the organization's mission from being disrupted and, if something bad happens, implementing an established plan to return to normal as quickly as possible.

If you accept this definition, the core components necessary to meet the objective of business continuity include a best-in-class capability to respond to a disruption quickly, communicate effectively, and ensure the recovery or continuation of IT services.

Many organizations and professionals generally group all of these efforts under one common umbrella: business continuity.

But if you've heard the term 'crisis management,' it is often used to align to the mission of managing the strategic response to the disruption. It also closely aligns to the organization's ability to communicate both internally and externally with key stakeholders.

And if you've heard the term 'IT disaster recovery' or simply 'disaster recovery,' this term, and the discipline associated with it, focuses on ensuring the continuity of or the recovery of IT services, including technical infrastructure, networks, applications, databases, data, and telephony.

Although it's common to group crisis management and IT disaster recovery as part of the broader business continuity effort, the creation and use of the resulting capabilities are driven by specialized resources and subdisciplines. Regardless, those organizations with best-in-class mitigation, response, and recovery capabilities carefully coordinate all preparedness/readiness efforts—sharing requirements, implementing solutions, exercising, and seeking continual improvement.

Chapter 41

Enjoy Your Job!

Because you're reading this book, you're probably at least partially responsible for business continuity at your organization. But here is the problem: Many people in your shoes aren't having much fun! How about you? Are you resigned to the idea that every day is a battle because many people just don't 'get' business continuity?

It doesn't have to be that way.

We believe that business continuity professionals should fight for the ability to say yes to the following statements:

1. I am empowered to make my organization resilient.
2. I have the resources needed to protect the organization as aligned to management's expectations.
3. I am challenged to grow personally and mature the program.
4. I enjoy my work.

If you can't say yes to the above statements, we suggest the following:

1. Don't accept the situation as it is! You have a *right* to these things—so fight for them!

2. This issue, like all others, is caused by weakness in at least one of the seven core elements. Decide which.

3. Strengthen those areas using the ideas in this book.

4. If you're stuck and nothing seems to be working, call me. I'll help you. My contact information is in the back of the book.

I hope you took away one key point from this book: ***Business continuity success is not driven solely by best-in-class methodology.*** Achieving the right level of resilience is often driven by excellent focus and engagement. When program managers establish the right connections by identifying key stakeholders, focusing on the right metrics, and acting on the right issues, all program participants feel more enthusiastic and connected with business continuity program objectives. The BCOS concepts discussed in this book are proven to positively evolve business continuity programs and help program managers achieve lasting engagement and improved outcomes, all leading to the appropriate level of resiliency—and their personal satisfaction.

Be sure to visit **castellanbc.com/felder** to access the additional resources mentioned throughout the book.

Also, we'd like to hear about your BCOS experiences. Email us your thoughts, feedback, and ideas on the BCOS to **bcos@castellanbc.com**.

A Little Background on the Felder Corporation

F elder Corporation is a contract manufacturer of pharmaceutical products. Universities, research labs, and even large pharmaceutical companies engage Felder to produce pharmaceutical products on their behalf. Some of the larger, global pharmaceutical companies are Felder's customers. Two of them alone account for 45 percent of Felder's $6B in annual revenue. Founded in 1990 and having gone public in 2003, Felder has performed in a profitable manner for five straight years, with operating margins averaging 18 percent. Over the past eighteen months, with the acquisition of one of its larger competitors, Belview Pharmaceuticals, Felder is operating close to capacity and facing several key decisions regarding expansion.

Despite Felder's large size, many employees would characterize it as fast-moving, risk-taking, and highly collaborative. One of the organization's key values that influences employee behavior is 'acting like an owner' by proactively taking ownership of continual improvement, innovation, and the customer experience. Above all else, the company obsesses about taking care of its people, its customers, and the patients it cares for. Knowledge-sharing is prevalent, and it's common to charter ad hoc teams to 'pitch in' to solve entrenched problems. Despite being a highly collaborative culture, the communication style is very direct and frequent.

Felder does not own any of the patents or formularies for the products it produces for clinical trials and commercial purposes. Rather, its customers are the ones investing and testing modern therapeutics. In 2015, Felder began offering additional services to its customers. Chief among them are process development (helping to create methods to develop, test, and commercialize therapies), adverse events reporting (helping to capture and manage when a patient has a negative reaction to a therapy), and clinical trials management (the controlled testing of

therapies among a select number of patients). To date, two customers have taken advantage of these services, which are run out of the Cleveland, Ohio, headquarters. Felder's organizational chart appears on the left.

While Felder intends to remain a contract manufacturer, the company is also evaluating a potential acquisition in which it would acquire the patents for three type 2 diabetes therapies. It is already producing one of these therapies in a contract manufacturing capacity. Independent of this acquisition, Felder plans to grow 18 percent annually through organic means over the next five years. The company has a strong pipeline of potential customers (with ongoing work from existing customers).

In the last calendar year, Felder manufactured twenty-nine different prescription pharmaceutical products for its eighteen global customers. Most of these products are produced at only one of its manufacturing locations. Each of its products is 'validated' by the FDA or another country's equivalent regulatory agency. This regulatory validation requires rigid supply chain, production, and quality processes executed to exacting standards. Each customer is responsible for seeking regulatory approval to market and sell these products. Therefore, Felder is unable to change or move production processes unless granted approval by both the FDA and the customer. Of the twenty-nine different products, Felder is the sole-source manufacturer for fifteen of these products.

Headquartered in Cleveland, Ohio, Felder has a total of seven manufacturing locations around the world:

- Independence, Ohio (USA)
- New Brunswick, New Jersey (USA)
- Concord, California (USA)
- Quincy, Massachusetts (USA)
- Portland, Oregon (USA)
- Carolina, Puerto Rico
- Cork, Ireland

Each site holds raw materials and warehouses finished goods onsite until the product is shipped to the customer or a distributor. Felder does not maintain a centralized distribution center in any of its markets.

Felder has a complex supply chain that includes single- and sole-source providers. Over the years, decisions to engage with a single provider for a product were made primarily for financial reasons, although in some cases, only one provider is available to supply a product.

Three years ago, Felder made the decision to implement SAP for many of its financial and operational processes. The SAP environment, together with many of the internal systems, runs 'in the cloud.' Felder also employs numerous SaaS applications. Nearly all its 'noncloud' and non-SaaS systems are located in one, third-party data center in Virginia, although its VOIP phone system is designed to be redundant across three sites (the Virginia data center, the Cleveland headquarters, and Concord).

During the last eight months, two of Felder's customers, including its largest customer, made inquiries regarding the company's business continuity capabilities. Although these two customers are making business continuity inquiries through the sales organization, all but two of Felder's customers have high-level contractual requirements mandating that Felder maintain a business continuity capability. Three of the customer contracts state that Felder must implement a business continuity program consistent with either the ISO 22301 or NFPA 1600 standards.

Because of the two customer inquiries, one of which indicates that Felder could be in breach of contract due to an inability to provide evidence of its business continuity capability, SVP of Business Development Steve Henry raised the issue with the senior leadership team at its most recent staff meeting.

The Fable's Key Participants

Key members of the senior leadership team are all based in Cleveland:

- CEO – Corey Smith
- CFO – Andrew Preston
- COO – Shannon Carter
- CIO – Anne Shoemaker
- SVP, Business Development – Steve Henry
- SVP, General Counsel – Jacob Cunningham
- VP, Marketing – Scott Patrick
- VP, Human Resources – Jack Tanner
- VP, Strategic Services – Melissa Zak
- VP, Risk Management – Michael Taylor
- VP, Internal Audit – Sara Terrence
- VP and General Manager, Puerto Rico – Robert Taverez

The four key players in Felder's business continuity journey include three senior leaders and a manager:

CFO – Andrew Preston. Andrew has been with Felder almost since its founding. In addition to his finance background, he has been in the pharmaceutical and biotechnology industry for most of his thirty-year career. He is well regarded among the senior leadership team at Felder for his knowledge of the business and its customers, and he's also one of the more risk-averse leaders. Andrew is a careful mix of strategic thinking and detail orientation. Risk management reports to him, and he's been assigned accountability for the business continuity program by the CEO.

VP, Risk Management – Michael Taylor (the book's narrator). Risk management, with responsibility for insurance and enterprise risk management (a newly chartered effort), reports into the CFO's organization. Michael is competent, responsible, and dependable and generally could be characterized as a hard-working executive. Although fairly new to the organization, he is already well respected among the members of the senior leadership team. As he's already experiencing, his job responsibilities pull him in many different directions, with competing demands on his time. His peers would not characterize him as terribly innovative, as he likes to do things the way they've always been done (just with better results). He's not easily accepting of change (and is sometimes described as dogmatic), and when unfamiliar with a topic, he often resists.

Manager, Quality – Ben Campbell. Ben is a manager in the quality department, with responsibility for quality engineering and quality control. He had responsibility for building a business continuity program for one of Felder's competitors. Five to ten years ago, he was well known in the business continuity industry as an innovative voice, before choosing to change career fields. Ben is friendly and approachable but reserved (not immediately forthcoming with information). He's intelligent, well-spoken,  and prefers a teaching approach that lets people learn by making mistakes. As a result, he is sometimes mischaracterized as being elusive because he often errs on the side of being vague, rarely giving direct answers.

COO – Shannon Carter. Shannon has been Felder's COO for three years, and she was a client of Michael Taylor's at her previous employer. Shannon has held senior roles at three pharmaceutical and biotech companies over the years, with her background primarily in manufacturing and supply chain. Shannon recruited Michael to come to Felder to 'fix' risk management, and she's been a great help in onboarding Michael to Felder's culture and executive leadership team.

About Castellan

As the largest global provider of business continuity and operational resilience solutions—spanning consulting, software, managed services, and staffing—Castellan is uniquely positioned to help clients find the right balance of risk tolerance and resilience to protect their employees, brand, and bottom line.

Leveraging a proprietary, proven process for driving business continuity success—the Business Continuity Operating System (BCOS)—Castellan partners with clients to establish a clear vision, drive real results, and provide on-going support from their community of business continuity experts.

Castellan helps clients replace uncertainty with confidence. Now you're ready.™

Headquartered in Audubon, PA, Castellan is strategically and financially backed by Resurgens Technology Partners, a technology-focused private equity firm based in Atlanta, GA.

Learn more at **castellanbc.com**.

About the Author

Brian Zawada is the chief operating officer for Castellan Solutions, the largest global provider of business continuity and operational resilience consulting, software, managed services, and staffing. Brian has more than twenty-five years of experience managing and building world-class, global business continuity programs that help organizations achieve and sustain the right level of resilience.

Outside of his work with Castellan and its clients, Brian previously served as the head of the United States Delegation to ISO Technical Committee 223, the authors of ISO 22301. Brian contributed to ISO 22301 and led the project team that created ISO 22317, the BIA standard, and ISO 22331, the business continuity strategy determination standard.

Brian is a frequent author and speaker, currently serving on the editorial advisory board of *Continuity Insights* magazine. Brian previously served as the Business Continuity Institute US Chapter board president and as the president of the Northern Ohio Chapter of the Association of Contingency Planners.

Brian is certified as a Fellow of the Business Continuity Institute.